A Grandmother Remembers

GROSSE ILE

OTHER PUBLICATIONS BY CARRAIG BOOKS

M. O Gallagher:	Saint Patrick's Quebec, 1824–1834
	Saint Brigid's Quebec, 1856–1981
	Grosse Ile Gateway to Canada, 1832–1938
	Grosse Ile , Porte d'Entrée du Canada, 1832–1938
James Mangan, F.S.C.	The Voyage of the Naparima
R. Clive Meredith	In All Weathers In all Seasons

Typesetting and Composition: Concept Danicom, Montreal

Cover Design: Éditions Marquis, Montmagny
Printed by Éditions Marquis, Montmagny

Copyright by Carraig Books 1989
Dépôt légal: Bibliothèque Nationale du Québec
Legal deposit: National Library of Canada
first trimester, 1989

ISBN 0-9690805-6-5

Jeannette Vekeman Masson

A Grandmother Remembers

GROSSE ILE

Translated from the French by
Johanne L. Massé

CARRAIG BOOKS
P. O. BOX 8733
STE-FOY, QUÉBEC
CANADA, G1V 4N6

TABLE OF CONTENTS

ACKNOWLEDGMENTS

My gratitude goes to Mr. Lucius Laliberté and Éditions Marquis Ltée of Montmagny.

I thank my daughter Rose Dompierre and Mrs. Louise de Cardaillac for seeing to the book's formatting. I also wish to thank my son-in-law, François Dompierre, my grandchildren, Dominique, Pascale, Julien, and Moïra Dompierre, as well as Carl Masson, Lynda and Lise Doyon, and Mr. Daniel Roberge for their precious help.

My thanks also to Freddy, Lucienne, and Annette Masson, Isidore Vekeman, Claire Enright, Rose and Dominique Dompierre who kindly lent me their photographs.

J.V.M.

My thanks in turn go to Jeannette Vekeman Masson who is happy to see her book reaching another sympathetic audience. To Johanne L. Massé, the translator, appreciation for the research and visits she made in order to get the spirit of the book. To Rose and François Dompierre for their care and interest as the translation proceeded, many thanks. To Ellen Clare O Gallagher and to Ken Wood for advice and help in bringing the book to light. To Éditions Marquis, thanks for collaboration in the use of the photos from the original. Thanks to Concept Danicom for patience during the process.

M. O G.
Carraig Books

EDITOR'S FOREWORD

It is a great pleasure to put another book about Grosse Ile into the hands of devotees of that dear island. Here a different aspect is presented, and a different period pictured than the often grim stories that the island usually elicits.

There was a debate among several of the first readers of the translation with regard to the unsophisticated air, or the lack of 'literary' grandeur of the new book. After reading this book, it is certain that the satisfied reader will agree with the translator, Johanne L. Massé, that this was not merely the communication of information, but a text whose style and form "are as important as its message."

"What makes Mrs. Masson's story so charming is its unpretentious, more-often-than-not conversational style which at once makes the reader feel as if he were in Mrs. Masson's home, sitting with her family and listening to her talk about her childhood. A more 'literary' translation of *Grandmaman* (or too 'literary' a translation of it) would jeopardize that relationship and be untrue to the French original. Such a rendering is, in my opinion, unjustifiable... I felt, that, given the identity of the narrator, Mrs. Masson, and her importance in the book, I had to preserve something of the French nature of the book. It is obvious that the story takes place in a French milieu and that the narrator is a native Francophone. It would appear artificial to have Mrs. Masson speak in other than the language of a native French speaker telling her story to English readers. Using this device, I was able to avoid awkward and tiresome translator's notes which would have disturbed the intimacy of the narrator-reader relationship. Case in point: the pun on 'graisse de roux' which I have Mrs. Masson explain in the text, as would a native Francophone writing in English, instead of using a translator's note."

Jeannettte Vekeman Masson's book paints a picture of an ordinary Quebec village on an extraordinary island. For immigrants during most of the nineteenth century and almost half of the twentieth century, this island was their first experience of Canadian soil.

It is to be hoped that the development of a national historic site now in the hands of Parks Canada will pay due tribute to the brave travelers and their gallant Canadian hosts.

Marianna O Gallagher
Publisher Editor
Quebec 1989

"*Sacred to the memory of thousands of Irish emigrants who, to preserve the Faith, suffered hunger and exile in 1847-48, and stricken with fever, ended here their sorrowful pilgrimage.*"

To my parents, Gustave Vekeman
Clara Rousseau
To my husband, Éméril Masson
To my children.

When one has loved
Time cannot erase the memories.

Jeannette Vekeman Masson

GROSSE ISLE

From the beguiling St. Lawrence, my noble Grosse Isle,
Ascends like incense, the rare perfume
Of your sturdy spruce pinnacles waving jubilantly
Despite the grey night falling on the spray.

Your heart remains fulfilled with glorious deeds
Inspired by divine and brotherly love
For the unfortunate sons of Ireland dying
Victims in the grip of the nefarious plague.

The cross of remembrance dominating the way
Tells the tearful pilgrim, kneeling on the ground
Where lowly clover sway beneath the vaulted sky,
Of death, the black angel, reaper of souls.

Dear Grosse Isle, land of my birth,
You evoke in me the dearest memories
Of my young years, when despite the storm,
I kept my heart as pure as the sweet zephyr.

Freddy Masson

November 1946

PREFACE

My dearest children,

You have asked me to describe Grosse Ile to you in all its aspects, to tell you about the way we lived there, to give you facts and details about everything and everybody. Well I think you will be satisfied.

While it is true that the soil of Grosse Ile holds the remains of hundreds and even thousands of immigrants, on its surface, along its enchanting shores, (south only, for the north shore has never been inhabited) has lived an entire population. It was made up of vigorous, courageous, and devoted people employed on the island to operate a quarantine station for immigrants arriving in Canada.

Your ancestors Masson and Vekeman lived on Grosse Ile. To tell you about them is to have you know and appreciate them. They were worthy, fair, courageous, and jovial men fully aware of their duties to their families as well as to their employer, the Government, regardless of which party was in power. One party often replaced the other, but the Massons were never replaced. They personified the work ethic. Those in power knew it and valued their presence. Four generations of Massons succeeded one another on the island over a period of a hundred and seventeen years. Although they did not reside on Grosse Ile as long, the Vekemans nevertheless left their mark. Your grandfathers, Johnny Masson and Gustave Vekeman, lived together on the island in true friendship. Today they lie side by side in their final resting place. They are the custodians of the past, and I hope, of the future.

Dearest children, I leave you the memory of your ancestors, men and women, as a precious legacy. Bear their names with pride, do them honor. Follow in their footsteps, leading upright and worthy lives.

When a head wind halts your progress or when you can't take advantage of the tide, do as the Grosse Ile sailors did: between gusts, beat to windward. You will still reach the shore. The island's skillful sailors knew how to sail into the wind.

If this document helps tighten the bonds of family and brotherly love amongst you, I shall be happy.

May all the descendants of the Massons and the Vekemans one day be reunited, not on Grosse Ile for it would surely be too small, but in the house of our Heavenly Father, the Ancestor of us all.

At the end of this book, you will find annexed a calendar of events pertaining to Grosse Ile from 1832 — when it became a quarantine station — to the present day.

If I am long-winded on certain subjects, it is because they have marked my life — and you did ask for details, so ...

Jeannette

GEOGRAPHIC POSITION OF GROSSE ILE

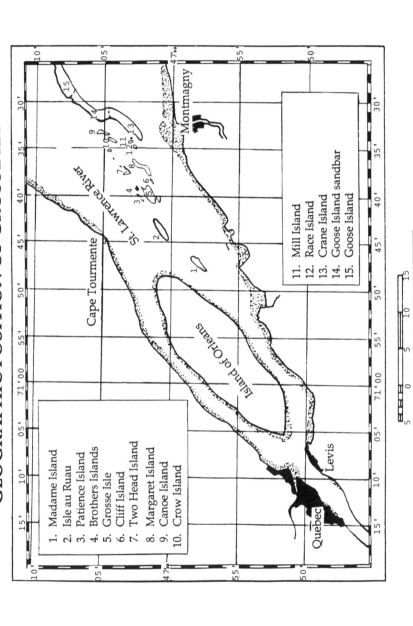

1. Madame Island
2. Isle au Ruau
3. Patience Island
4. Brothers Islands
5. Grosse Isle
6. Cliff Island
7. Two Head Island
8. Margaret Island
9. Canoe Island
10. Crow Island

11. Mill Island
12. Race Island
13. Crane Island
14. Goose Island sandbar
15. Goose Island

St. Lawrence River

Cape Tourmente

Island of Orleans

Montmagny

Quebec

Levis

No. 2 Ruau is the island owned by Dr. Geoge Douglas, and the scene of his death.

No. 6 Ile la Sottise – the French word means the silly one, or in popular parlance, 'the drunk'. The name may have come from ships which tried to get past the island without stopping and ended up on the reefs, hence, with a drunk for a captain. There is another tradition that the word, pronounced 'Sottees', might be a distortion of the English word Southeast. The English name is hardly as interesting! The island is southeast of Grosse Ile.

No. 13 Crane Island once had the seigneurie of Alexander Macpherson Lemoyne, the Quebec historian.

Nos. 5 and 8. The anchorage lay between Grosse Ile and Ile Marguerite in the period before the wharf was built.

Ed. Note: These names changed frequently in popular usage. Different maps at different periods use different names.

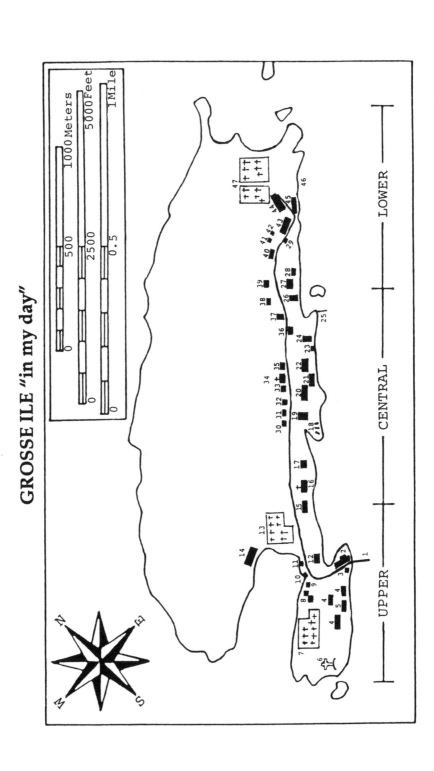

GROSSE ILE "in my day"

GROSSE ILE "in my day"

1. Upper wharf
2. Dynamo, pump, showers
3. Guardian's house
4. Hotels for immigrants
5. Plumber's shop
6. Irish monument
7. Upper cemetery
8. Disinfection sheds
9. Electrician's house
10. Maternity hospital
11. Guard house
12. Dr. Heylen's house
13. Cemetery
14. Upper block
15. Protestant presbytery
16. Protestant chapel
17. Government hotel
18. Battery
19. Dr. Martineau's house
20. Center block
21. Common stable
22. Public Works house
23. Marconi Station
24. Dr. Côté's house

25. Lower wharf
26. Dr. Heagerty's house
27. Pit Masson's house
28. Pit Masson's stable
29. Isolation house
30. Dr. Martineau's gardener's house
31. Dr. Martineau's coach house
32. Wood shed
33. Post office
34. Catholic chapel
35. Catholic presbytery
36. School
37. Johnny Masson's house and bakery
38. Laboratory
39. Nurses' residence
40. Jos Brautigam's house
41. Oil storage shed
42. Straw storage barn
43. Hospital
44. Typhus sheds or "No. 4"
45. Lower block
46. "Little pebble sand"
47. Cemeteries

SETTING

Geographically, Grosse Ile is situated twenty-nine miles from Quebec City. It lies downriver from Ile d'Orléans, Ile Madame, and Ile au Ruau. Topographically speaking, it is 1.805 miles long, 0.623 mile wide and oh! so very picturesque!

Its terrain is uneven. Its grassy or bushy hollows and its wooded areas are pierced here and there by bare or mossy jutting rocks. On the south side, a ridge of rock extends lengthwise across the island for some distance. The Catholic chapel and several houses stand against it. Everywhere you look the scenery is beautiful.

The contour of the island is well outlined by coves and by the famous "upper" headland on which stands the Irish memorial. And then there are the two wharfs and also the beautiful beach that my brothers and I had named "the little pebble sand." How often we played there as children. Beyond, toward the "lower" end of the island, the shore is strewn with huge flat stones well polished by the tide. Farther down along the water's edge, at the tip of the island, lies a mile-long stretch of tideland where rushes and eelgrass grow. The north shore is steeper and more rugged.

As you can see, we were not living on a barren, windswept rock. On the contrary, Grosse Ile was beautiful. The scenery was breathtaking and never monotonous with, as its backdrop, the river's two shores fading on the horizon beyond Cap Tourmente to the north and Montmagny to the south.

The ever changing river with its twice daily rising and ebbing tide added to the charm. On fair summer days, its mirrorlike surface reflected the sky's blue, and schools of porpoises came to play around the island. They expelled jets of water like the whales in our picture books. When they surfaced, their white backs gleamed in the sun.

It was a fascinating sight to behold. I sat and watched them at play many a time from the rocks in front of my house. But they have long since disappeared, even near Ile aux Coudres where they once abounded. People no longer fish for bass nor tomcod in those parts. Why did they all disappear? Nobody knows!

On stormy days, the river was majestic and intimidating. Hurled by the raging wind, huge waves came thunderously crashing on the rocks, the river pouring out its heart at our feet. I could listen to it tirelessly, trying to understand it. I was occasionally so immersed in its sounds, it seemed that the river and I were but one.

There were always liners, schooners, and white-sailed light craft furrowing the river. Thus it outlined its history and served as a link between different worlds.

Like a mother hen amidst her chicks, Grosse Ile was surrounded by little islands which were readily accessible by sailboat or rowboat. Your father Éméril often visited them.

We sometimes went, of an evening, to Ile Sainte-Marguerite where lived only the family of Odilon Pruneau. Mrs. Pruneau was Johnny Masson's sister. We would go down with the ebbing tide and return with the rising. The moonlight was fascinating; the river was ours. Joe Lachance of Ile au Canot used to say, "The river is a god to us."

I shall never forget these St. Lawrence islands that we the Vekeman children used to call "the little blue islands." They were my childhood delight, and I have thrived upon my memories of them.

I often see myself again by the water's edge, my back against the burning rocks in the sun, drinking in the sight of the river and its islands. No matter what the weather was like, the farthest of these islands always appeared blue. They were gracefully wrapped in a slight veil of mist.

For me they marked the boundary between my world and the other. Beyond those "little blue islands" lay an unknown world from whence a ship would suddenly emerge. It carried men whose customs and language differed from mine.

My little blue islands

I spent countless hours trying to understand the world's mysteries: earth, water, and sky. Once in a while, for a fraction of a second — or was it an eternity? — I would unravel the mystery. I was awestruck, and my child's soul burst with all that beauty. I was in love with life, with my islands, and with my days.

What can I say about the gulls and the white mews which flew over the river high in the sky? Suddenly, having spotted a fish, they would dive for it at a dizzying speed then fly back to their nest to share their catch with their little ones.

The island's rich alluvial soil provided a diverse and luxuriant vegetation: maple, oak, birch, linden, elm, pine, spruce, fir, eastern hemlock, yellow birch, cherry tree, hawthorn, hazel, American yew, pembina (cranberry-tree), juniper, gooseberry and raspberry bushes, elder, and currant bushes but hardly any wild strawberry or blueberry bushes.

Flowers in every color of the rainbow abounded: blue flags, white daisies, buttercups, bellflowers, butter-and-eggs, columbines, violets, willow herbs, wild pansies, tiny white flowers with a sweet and pervasive fragrance, forget-me-nots, wild lilies of the valley, jasmines, strings of pungent pink florets shaped like bells, and wild roses.

All those flowers, how could I not remember them?

Spring brought crocuses, bloodroots — which we called redroots — Dutchman's breeches, lilies, white and red trilliums, bearberries, various species of ferns, horsetails, and clover.

I will spare you the long list of forage plants — or weeds as we call them when they grow in our gardens! Everlastings, milkweed; some I forget, others I will skip. I remember how the vines and hops, entwined about some of the large trees here and there, brought their own poetry to the scene. When I was young, during the month of May, I made many beautiful bouquets, at our pastor's request, to decorate the altar of the Blessed Virgin.

This profusion of vegetation and of nectar-filled flowers attracted some birds and insects including bees, wasps, bumblebees, and so on. As we used to run around barefoot when we were young, we often got stung by wasps, stepping heedlessly on a nest hidden in the grass.

The birds? Apart from the gulls and mews, there were of course crows! As well as a few owls, small chickadees, goldfinches, songbirds whose names I do not know, and hummingbirds of brilliant green hues. These hummingbirds truly looked like winged emeralds, enthusiastically gathering nectar from the flowers' chalices with their long bills. They were quite tame. Many a time, in the summerhouse Papa had built in our garden, my brother Gustave captured them in his tiny hands to admire them up close and then to release them.

Amidst those birds flew butterflies. Brightly colored butterflies, big and small.

At low tide, the bare muddy clay of the beaches was put to good use by numerous swallows. They used it to build nests, gathered together in colonies and separated from each other by party walls. Swallows demonstrate a sense of sociability and thrift. I spent much time watching them at work. They would deposit beakfuls of clay, layer by layer, smooth it with their bills, and let it harden in the sun.

Before leaving in the fall, they would alight by the hundreds on the power lines which bowed under the strain of their combined weight. Then they would gracefully fly away describing arabesques. It was as if they were skywriting their farewells before leaving us.

Also, in the spring, the joyful call of the Canada geese heralded the coming of the fair season even though there was still ice floating on the river. In the fall, their shrill honks "a a oot" (which to our French ears sounded like "en route" — let's go) meant that they were rallying for the journey south. They paraded across the sky by the thousands.

There was no game such as foxes or hares on the island, except for the two foxes sighted in 1905 and 1906. At one time, there were some rats, brought by the schooners which carried our firewood, and some bedbugs, imported from Europe — if you please!— by the immigrants. Traps, disinfectants, and hygiene, however, soon rid the island of those intruders.

Dear children, you now have some idea of the setting — the environment in which the people of Grosse Ile lived. Have I told you enough to convince you that life on Grosse Ile was not boring but rather most enriching for those who knew how to appreciate the beauty which God had bestowed upon this island?

POPULATION

MEANS OF COMMUNICATION

Who were the inhabitants of Grosse Ile? And what did these people do?

Grosse Ile had been a quarantine station since 1832. Immigrants coming to Canada were detained on the island by the Department of Agriculture so they could be treated, cured, or kept under observation if they carried any disease. The quarantine did not necessarily last forty days. The sick, and everyone who had been in contact with them, had to stay on the island until there was no longer any risk of contagion.

It must be said that over a hundred and thirty-five years ago, immigrants already weakened by poverty and famine — then rampant throughout Europe and particularly in Ireland — fled to Canada in hopes of finding the promised land. They came aboard sailing ships on which comfort and hygiene were unknown, especially on the decks and in the holds where the poor, steerage passengers were jammed. These people often became sick during the voyage, which then lasted from one to two months — and sometimes longer — depending on the size of the ship.

These boats were a far cry from modern passenger ships. Several sick passengers would sometimes die on board. Put in sacks, their bodies were simply thrown into the ocean with a prayer. Those who managed to survive were landed on Grosse Ile.

A highly qualified personnel was obviously needed on the island to take care of all those people. In my day, there were:

- a chief medical officer (superintendent of the island)
- a secretary for the chief medical officer
- three assistant medical officers
- four nurses
- two interpreters
- two cooks
- a laundress
- an engineer in charge of disinfecting operations
- an administrator to take care of hospital personnel, record keeping, and accounting
- three handymen for maintenance work at the hospital
- a baker
- a plumber
- a carpenter
- a carter-ambulance driver
- an assistant carter-ambulance driver
- two electricians
- two constables
- a telegrapher
- two wireless operators for the Marconi station where Henri Masson (Éméril's brother) worked
- a teacher
- a Catholic priest
- a Protestant chaplain
- And manning each of the two boats — the *Alice* and the *Polana* (later renamed the *Jalobert*):
- a captain
- a mate
- a bowman-helmsman
- a greaser
- two stokers
- three seamen
- a cook

Most of those people were summer employees. As the quarantine station on Grosse Ile officially opened on the first of April and closed on November 25, that was a rather long summer! Several of these seasonal employees came with their families, so the population numbered about 250 people.

There were in addition, depending on the year, from ten to thirty public works employees. These men came to construct and repair buildings. They did not bring their families, but lived in a camp supervised by a foreman. They spent only two months on the island.

And there were, of course, the immigrants. The sick were hospitalized, while those under observation stayed in a clinic hotel built especially for them.

Four ships provided transportation for all those people: the *Alice*, the *Polona*, a yacht, and an ice canoe.

The steamboat *Alice*, named in honor of Mrs. Martineau, the superintendent's wife, carried the islanders to and from Quebec. Its number was 122260. It was 125.5 feet long, 25.8 feet wide, and 10.85 feet deep.

The *Alice* replaced the *Contest* on June 20, 1907. The *Contest* was one of those ancient, white sidewheelers with a walking beam. We used to refer to those beams as "cigars."

The steamer *Alice* at the islanders' disposal from 1907 on

During the summer, the yacht was used to cross over to Montmagny. This vessel was twenty feet long and propelled by a motor and sails. Besides the three crew members, it could carry two or three passengers.

The ice canoe was used to convey the mail from Montmagny during the winter, as well as the doctor when he was needed.

Those three ships provided transportation for the islanders. For the immigrants, there was the *Polana*. This steamer was one hundred and seven feet long, twenty-three feet wide, and twelve feet deep. In 1911, it took the place of the *Challenger*, a dauntless little boat which later served as a tug in Quebec harbor.

I do not know what kind of boat transported the immigrants before the *Challenger* came into service. But I do know that around 1870, when your great-grandfather Édouard Masson arrived on the island, there was a very large flat-bottomed boat propelled by oars and sails, similar to those used to ferry cows in the region of the Sorel islands and called *"chaloupe à vache."*

It was in this boat that the sick were brought ashore from the big ships. When the weather was rough, the men probably had to drop anchor and wait. On a heavy sea, it was no small task to get those poor, sick creatures down rope ladders hanging along the hulls of big schooners or sailing boats.

To carry the immigrants, there was the *Polana*.

But with more imposing ocean steamers and a bigger boat to carry the sick ashore, sturdier, more rigid gangways came to be used. Transshipment then became easier for everyone. There have been heroic times for the immigrants and the island employees.

Grosse Ile boasted a Marconi station, a telegraph office, and an internal telephone network. Our phones were those ancient, big boxes — have you ever seen one? Dr. Martineau's phone was connected to the hospital's and to that of every house on the island.

This phone, in the entrance hall of the "upper" hotel, is still part of the island's internal communication network.

In my day, an icebreaker owned by the government, the *Lady Grey* more often than not, arrived from Quebec at the end of March. The medical superintendent, then Dr. Martineau, was coming to officially open the quarantine season and to make sure that everything was in order and that every department was ready to start operating again. It was the duty of those who stayed on Grosse Ile through the winter to keep the facilities of the station in good condition.

The *Lady Grey* came down from Quebec at the end of March
to open the quarantine season.

Mrs. Martineau always made that first trip of the season with her
husband and came to visit the school. And she would give us the rest of the
day off! The *Alice* and the *Polana* would only arrive a few days later, between
April 5 and 15, when the St. Lawrence was relatively free of ice.

In the spring, a sheet of ice, six to eight feet thick, surrounded the
wharfs. Equipped with axes, the men had to clear away the better part of it.
After the ships had arrived, the crews would finish the job with jets of hot
water. In 1911, the assistant carter drowned while clearing away the ice.

Preparing for the officials' arrival, the employees who had wintered
on the island had to clear a path from the lower to the upper wharf. Since no
path was kept open during the winter, that meant a lot of snow to shovel.
The men opened up a deep trench in the snow, and we the children had a lot
of fun jumping across it. It was quite an event when the men started clearing
the path. We would follow the progress of their work with great interest. It
was just as fascinating for us as it is for hockey fans today to follow the play-
offs!

Thus stirred, the snow rapidly melted, and the path was soon dry.
This foreshadowed the return of fair weather, renewed life, and more nu-
merous — often new — classmates. But for us the children, every day on
Grosse Ile was sunny, be it winter or summer.

In the fall, the station closed on November 25, and along with the Canada geese, the doctors, the nurses, the constables, the electricians, the Protestant minister, and the others left. All these people departed on the last voyage of the *Alice* and the *Polana*.

Only about a dozen families remained on the island — no more than were needed to ensure its maintenance. The population then comprised sixty people: twenty-seven adults (including the teacher and the Catholic priest), fifteen school children, and eighteen younger children. These were the figures in 1911.

The Marconi station snugly wrapped in a white blanket of snow

Interpreters also had to leave the island since they were no longer needed. Papa, who was 65 years old — today's retirement age — was less than pleased with all that moving back and forth. So he had taken the job on condition that we winter on the island with the same advantages as the caretakers — free heating, free lighting, and free rent. Unlike the caretakers, Papa did not of course get paid during the four winter months, and in the beginning, he did not earn much (sixty dollars a month). But interpreters were rather hard to find eighty years ago, so the government agreed to Papa's request.

When the ships left, all those who remained on the island would be standing on the wharf to see the others off. We would stand there and wave as long as we could see the people. The boat would then suddenly become a dark spot on the water, and we would slowly make for home. We the children walked back with the carefree spirit of youth, but what about our parents?

LODGINGS

How were the inhabitants of Grosse Ile housed?

Very well, very well indeed, and a lot better than you could have imagined. In fact some of you had a chance to judge for yourselves when we visited the island in 1974.

In the 19th century — around 1832-1850, I would say — there were but a few houses on Grosse Ile. Those houses were small, low-roofed, and thus easier to heat. Though plain, they were rather comfortable for the time. They were old Canadian-style whitewashed board and batten houses, a few specimens of which can still be seen between Trois-Rivières and Quebec.

All — or nearly all of those houses were later torn down. The oldest one was still standing in 1906 when we the Vekemans arrived on Grosse Ile. Your grandfather Johnny Masson lived in that house during the summer, and it is there that I caught my first glimpse of your father, Éméril Masson. Our Heavenly Father was then no doubt setting the wheels of our destiny in motion, without our knowing it for we were only seven years old.

Little house I so often recall — wrapped in mystery!

At first, the government had to remedy some urgent and dramatic situations. In time, however, they organized the islanders' lives well.

I cannot say exactly when — probably around 1880-1900 — two rows of houses were built for the summer employees: one of six houses in the lower section and one of eight in the central section. Another eight-house row was put up, between 1903 and 1906, in the upper section. We used to call it "the new houses."

Those lodgings were spacious. In the lower row, each house boasted seven rooms: a kitchen, a sitting room, and a bedroom downstairs; four bedrooms plus a bathroom upstairs. In the other two rows, each house comprised eight rooms: four downstairs and four upstairs, plus a bathroom.

We lived in the lower row, opposite the "No. 4."
On the left, Pit Masson and his cart.

In those days, houses were built not only by hand but also with care. It was a labor of love and pride in a job well done. Houses were then sturdy and warm. Inside, the houses on Grosse Ile were carefully finished with roughcast — because it was then in fashion — but roughcast which was never cast off! The whole interior was initially painted white, but we could change the color if we pleased.

Mother had wallpapered our sitting room. A varnished hardwood wainscot covered the lower part of the walls. The kitchen boasted beautiful, roomy cabinets and a closet. On the outside, those buildings were sided with horizontal boards painted beige. The roofs were covered with black shingles. Those were well-fitted shingles, for to my knowledge, the roofs never leaked be it on rainy days or during the thaw.

Each row of houses was fitted with winter sashes, storm windows, and big, sturdy chimneys which drew well and were large enough for Santa Claus to go through! The foundations were thick, and nothing froze in the basements during the winter because the inner walls and the floor were of cement.

The three rows had summer kitchens standing about twenty feet away from them. Those kitchens were housed in either three or four sheds. Carefully finished inside as well as outside, they were gabled and painted the same color as the main building. Each shed housed two kitchens separated by a party wall and each with its own door. During the winter, these summer kitchens were used as cold storage for our supply of meat — beef, pork, poultry, and fish. A section of the shed served to keep our firewood dry.

The upper row boasted eight large houses which we called the "new houses."

The back of the central row and the summer kitchens

Each row of houses also had its own privy. Very well built, with a pointed roof and painted the same color as the houses inside and out. Watertight, it did not let snow in during the winter. And most thoughtful of all, a bench just the right height for children! Each toilet was of course separated from the next by a partition. It was not a shabby construction built just any old way. On the contrary, nicely finished, with paneled doors and sturdy door handles, it looked very nice indeed. Until 1909, we had running water only in the summer. That explains why there were so many privies!

Almost all the employees who stayed on the island yearlong had their own individual family houses, as did the doctors although they did not winter there. All those houses were beautiful, each different from the others, painted white with dark green frames and roofs — except Dr. Côté's and Dr. Heagerty's which were made of brick. Those houses still remain on Grosse Ile today.

Dr. Heylen had to go inspect all ships upon their arrival off the island. His house was built near the wharf where the *Polana* was on standby.

Dr. Martineau, the station's superintendent, standing on his veranda in 1911. This beautiful house burned down in 1925.

Our neighbors, Jos Brautigam's family

We the Vekemans occupied the last house of the lower row. A large family had lived there before us. To give them more space, a kitchen with two bedrooms above it had been added. Going from the main house to the kitchen, we had to go down one step. This addition had no foundations. The ground, so close to the river, began to slope at the far end of the kitchen, so much so that the end of the addition stood on piles. There was a huge stove (with a beaver engraved on the oven door) to cook our food and heat those three rooms. A two-step stove kept the rest of our house warm during the winter.

Pit Masson's house

Dr. Côté's house which later became that of the island superintendent. Freddy Masson lived there until 1980.

Dr. Heagerty's house

In the early days of the quarantine station, people had to use oil lamps, draw drinking water from wells, and use the river water for washing. Then around the end of the 19th century, a generator was installed in the upper end of Grosse Ile. It pumped water up to a huge tank standing on the Irish memorial headland. This system provided good water pressure.

Each house had its own tank in the attic. In the evening, the children had fun taking turns at the pump to fill it up for the next day. In each kitchen, there was a small, vertical cast iron tank like those one can still see in the old sections of Quebec. Part of the piping connected to it passed through the wood stove. When the stove was burning, we had hot water. Needless to say that there was no shortage of hot water throughout the winter!

The generator also supplied electricity for the entire island from seven p.m. to midnight. We put away our oil lamps, but never for good because — for some reason I never knew — the power was shut off at midnight. The electricity was also cut off when the station was closed from November 25 to April first. So on winter evenings and when needed, we still had to use good old oil lamps. The hospital was also equipped with an acetylene lighting system.

When I was very young, around 1912 or maybe earlier, I remember that on summer evenings the women did their ironing with electric irons. You can see that we were ahead of our time on Grosse Ile. It was not until much later that many large villages and rural areas of the *Belle Province* were electrified.

From the upper wharf to the lower hospital, huge lamps mounted on high poles lighted the island. So there was no way ghosts and spirits could wander around at night because it was too bright!

The generator supplied electricity for the entire island.

A dirt road, 1.5 miles long, ran across the island from the upper wharf to a point not far beyond the lower hospital. To the delight of pedestrians, a boardwalk, two or even three planks wide, had been built along two thirds of this road. In 1913, a section of the boardwalk, between Johnny Masson's house and Dr. Martineau's, was replaced by a three-foot wide cement sidewalk.

An island being an island, isolated from the rest of the world, the government probably saw fit — with reason — to encourage people to come and work there by providing their employees with all possible comforts. It was thus easier to recruit personnel. Grosse Ile was certainly as comfortable as Robinson Crusoe's island!

Ultimate luxury for the pedestrians, a boardwalk

FOOD SUPPLIES

Breathtaking scenery and comfortable houses do not, however, put food on the table. What did the people eat? And where did they get their food supplies? They simply crossed the river just as Christopher Columbus crossed the ocean to come to America!

On Mondays and Thursdays, the sail and motor yacht of my day — way earlier it must have been only a sail and rowboat — would cross over to Montmagny to fetch the mail and the documents needed by the superintendent. It also brought supplies, perishable goods, and most importantly, fresh meat for the hospital and the islanders who had given their orders to the captain. There were four icehouses on the island: one in each of the lower, central, and upper sections and one for the hospital. They were large icehouses, with sawdust-insulated walls, filled with large ice blocks. Built in the middle of small groves, they stood in the shade all day. They enabled us to keep meat from Monday till Thursday, Thursday till Saturday, and Saturday till the next Monday. Get the picture?

Moreover, twice a week, the steamer *Alice* went up to Quebec, on Tuesdays to buy fresh meat for the hospital and on Saturdays to fetch the large orders. The superintendent went along once a week to report to the office of the Department of Agriculture.

The inhabitants of Grosse Ile also traveled to Quebec once in a while, especially mothers, since the employees could hardly leave their work. When the latter did make the trip, however, they had to wear their uniforms. The uniform was mandatory for all Grosse Ile employees, except the public works men.

And how did we pay? We had everything charged, and at the end of the month, each employee received his paycheck from the government. Nothing to compare with today's big salaries, but it was a steady income. The husband or the wife would then have the check cashed by the supplier, who kept his due, and everybody was happy. We bought mainly from lower-town merchants near the wharfs: grocer, butcher, shoemaker, general merchant, etc. They were all proud as peacocks to do business with Grosse Ile residents.

Although the salaries were not much, money was still worth something in those days; and the Grosse Ile employees paid neither rent, lighting, firewood nor oil for the lamps in winter. Nor did they pay the doctor for delivering babies and taking care of illnesses commonly treated on the island — such as ship fever, scarlet fever, smallpox, diphtheria, and measles — burns, cuts, tonsil removals, and bandages. Cough syrup and ointments were also provided free. For major surgery, one had to go to Quebec. I remember thinking that the Bayer cross on headache tablets looked funny. It has been around for a long time!

We did not pay for passage to Montmagny or Quebec. But we had to report to the medical superintendent before leaving the island. During quarantines, hospital employees and their families were not allowed to leave the island. That only made sense. They would then give their lists of errands to the captain of the *Alice*. The crews of both steamers always remained on board ship.

The hospital store supplied us with pillows, wool blankets, single iron bedsteads, and straw mattresses, free of charge. We the Vekemans had never slept on straw mattresses before coming to Grosse Ile. How comfortable they were! In a pinch, we could also obtain such goods as tea, coffee, or oatmeal, provided we paid for them.

We were entitled to ax handles and straw, of which a large shed was always filled to capacity. Straw and bundled hay came from Ile aux Grues. The *Alice* went all the way down to Rocher Rouge to meet the schooners from Ile aux Grues. The crewmen then transshipped the cargo. The schooners from Ile aux Grues did not come all the way to Grosse Ile's lower wharf. The spray would have made the hay and straw wet. Bigger and with bulwarks, the *Alice* provided a better protection for this cargo.

Maintenance services for the houses — plumbing, carpentry, electricity, chimney sweeping, inside and outside painting once in a while — were free. Everyone could keep chickens, fatten a pig or two, and make a small garden as long as it was well fenced in because of the cows.

When there were a lot of immigrants, it was sometimes impossible to get enough fresh milk every day for the islanders and the hospital's patients. So those who wintered on the island kept a cow or two, but never more to give everyone a fair chance because we all had to supply the hospital with as much milk as it needed, and the government paid five cents a quart for it!

When there were few immigrants at the hospital, the children drank wholesome milk to their hearts' content and people skimmed the milk jugs with a spoon. Later on, some bought small separators and made delicious butter.

Jos Brautigam's healthy family in their garden

Pit Masson's beautiful garden

Cows roamed freely and grazed all over the island. They ate all sorts of forage plants, so the fields and the sides of the road were always well kept. At low tide, their menu included rushes from the shores, which contained some iodine and salt. They could drink their fill of water, which made them good milkers. They gave rich, wholesome milk — not "city" milk. Three communal stables provided shelter for them in winter.

In the fall we put aside a few dozen eggs. We kept them in the pantry, wrapped in paper. We gathered in the vegetables in our gardens. Those who left Grosse Ile in the fall or manned the ships had neither gardens nor animals. In June, around St. John the Baptist Day, the *Alice* would stop at Ile d'Orléans on her way back from Quebec, and the women would stock up on strawberries. They were not expensive then. For about two dollars, we got enough to feed an army. We turned them into delicious jam. Then in November, the wives would go to Quebec and spend the October paycheck stocking up for the winter.

Here is approximately what they would buy:
    One hundred pounds of white sugar
    Fifty pounds of brown sugar
    Fifty pounds of dried white beans
    Fifty pounds of dried peas
    One peck of apples
    Five gallons of molasses (grandfather Johnny bought a peck)
    One-half bushel of coarse salt to salt down the fat of the pigs
        fattened during the summer
    Tea
    Coffee
    Oatmeal
    Rice
    "Village" brand cookies
    Raisins to bake pies
    Dried apples
    Powdered chocolate
    Spices and the like
    Vermicelli
    Macaroni
    Oranges came by way of Montmagny in winter, and we en-
        joyed them only during the Holiday season.
    Flour and bread we bought directly from Johnny Masson's
        bakery.
    There was also a good supply of walnuts, filberts, almonds in
        shell, Brazil nuts, and peanuts in shell.

Add to that one or two mysterious packages concealed from us the children. They contained sweets for Christmas. We never saw them come into the house. I believe the parents — mine at least — conspired with Pit Masson who delivered those packages while we were at school. As for our Christmas presents, our parents probably bought them during a visit to Quebec in the summer and hid them in the fireplace until Santa came.

Our parents put November's paycheck aside for unforeseen expenses which might arise during the winter.

We also had fish. Johnny Masson owned a rowboat for his own enjoyment. He and Éméril often went fishing and many a time came back with miraculous catches. They gave or sold those fish to anyone who wanted some.

A miraculous catch! From left to right: Johnny Masson, Éméril, Baptiste Morin, Odilon Pruneau, and Georges Masson. The net in Johnny's boat was made by Johnny and Éméril.

When he was young, Éméril made fishing nets with his father. They used no. 9 cord; just imagine their long and painstaking labor. One winter, they used one hundred and fifty pounds of line! To fish for sardines, they made nets with very fine meshes. But they also used hooks. For sardine fishing, they made them out of sewing needles, though the women objected. I too often made fish hooks for my brothers. I would stick a needle in a cork, heat its sharp-pointed end with a candle, then bend it with pliers, and that was it!

I almost forgot — the employees were also entitled, every year, to a suit and a pair of shoes, and every other year, to a knee-length woolen overcoat, a raincoat, and a sou'wester (a sort of waterproof "fireman's" hat whose name the children pronounced "sawest"). Those things helped to make ends meet. Papa rarely wore out his shoes. When he did not need the boots the government provided, he traded them to a shoemaker near the wharfs in Quebec for two pairs of children's boots.

UNIFORMS FOR MEDICAL OFFICERS

OF THE CANADIAN QUARANTINE SERVICE

1911

Cap. — *The cap to be of the pattern approved already by the Honourable the Minister of Agriculture, the issue of which to the officers commenced four years ago. These caps to be supplied by J.B. Laliberté, Quebec, Que., on requisition from the Office of the Director-General of Public Health.*

Coat. — *The coat to be a four-button double-breasted sack, with new Crown brass buttons.*

Vest. — *The vest to be single-breasted, without a collar, with six uniform buttons.*

Trousers. — *The trousers to be made in fashionable style.*

Overcoat. — *Greatcoats to be double-breasted, full length, with storm collar, and new Crown brass buttons front and back; and to be made loose, with strap as well as buttons at back.*

Material. — *Coat, vest and trousers to be made of fine blue-black twilled worsted serge; the overcoat of heavy dark blue frieze.*

Buttons. — *The buttons will be supplied from the Office of the Director-General at Ottawa, and will be furnished by N. Scully and E.J. Scott (see attached memorandum marked "Buttons"). These buttons are stamped "Quarantine, Canada".*

Boots. — *One pair of black leather boots to be allowed each Officer per annum, price not to exceed $5.00.*

Gold Braid — *etc., around sleeves. There should be around the sleeves at the wrist of both coat and overcoat gold lace and scarlet velvet as follows: For a Medical Superintendent or Head Medical Officer, three separate circles of gold lace, with loop, and a scarlet velvet band between these circles of lace. Where there is an assistant medical officer at a station, his uniform should have two circles of gold lace, with loop, and a scarlet band between these circles of lace.* [1]

A few quarantine station employees in uniform. On the right, my father.

---

[1] Original of a memorandum approved by the Minister of Agriculture and signed by J. Montizambert, M.D. Director-General of Public Health, May 30, 1911.

"But we were never afraid on the river; we knew it and it knew us. We treated each other with respect." Éméril.

HEATING

WINTER PREPARATIONS

CROSSING AMIDST THE ICE FLOES

Heating was paid for by the government. Sometime during the summer, the schooners of the Desgagnés from the north shore (somewhere in or around Les Éboulements) brought a supply of wood for the coming winter: four cords of good hardwood — maple and yellow birch — and eight to ten cords, I do not remember exactly, of softwood — spruce and fir — for each family wintering on the island, as well as a common stock of softwood for everyone to use during the summer. The hospital and the school had coal heating.

We used the softwood for the kitchen stoves. The provision needed by each family was cut in four-foot long pieces by means of a circular saw. The saw was driven by a big, coal-fueled steam engine. We the children called it "blockgine." The men said "block-engine" — an engine mounted on a platform equipped with wheels. It smoked like a locomotive and went "puff, puff." It was later replaced by a smaller engine. The carter used his horses to bring the engine — big or small — to the house of each family for the wood-cutting bee.

That was another big event for us the children. We were allowed to watch, but from a distance. It was fascinating for us to see how skillfully the men put the logs on the saw bench and cut them into short lengths, all without cutting off their fingers!

We listened spellbound to the high-pitched sound of the saw biting into the wood: a long "whee" and the hesitating "puff, puff" of the big engine, later replaced by the faster "tuff, tuff" of the small one.

Once the wood was cut, we were somewhat less enthusiastic. It fell mainly to the children to store the kindling wood in the shed to shelter it from the snow. That way we always had some dry wood for the kitchen stove. The long hardwood logs to fuel the two-step stove remained outside. In winter, we had to shovel the snow to get them. That was no picnic, believe me! But to roll yourself in the snowdrifts until you were so cold your ears, nose, and fingers were about ready to break off, that was fun. *That* was called playing outside in the fresh air!

The men carefully gathered the sawdust to insulate the icehouses. They replaced the sawdust every year, so the icehouses were always very clean and fresh-smelling.

So the matter of heating was taken care of and we did not have to worry about it. Once we had stocked up on food, we were ready for the snow.

During the first week of December, the men slaughtered the pigs fattened during the summer. The cold had set in by then, so the meat froze. It was rather hard, tiring, and cold for the butchers, but they had brought their antifreeze — gin! — beforehand. Although the meat froze, I do not remember one single man ever freezing! They did not overdo it though — Grosse Ile was the island of the "Wise."

The women, in their kitchens, needed patience rather than antifreeze. Surrounded by children who wanted to touch everything, they prepared blood pudding, sausages, "cretons," leaf lard, headcheese, and meat pies. They put the choicest cuts of pork to freeze in the summer kitchens, and the pieces of fat in salting tubs.

When winter and the northeast storms came, we were ready for them. There were no material cares nor worries for the parents. Then for the children there began a period of dreaming and hoping. Christmas was fast approaching.

You see that as far as lodging, food, and heating — in short, material things — were concerned, the people were rather well off on Grosse Ile. Papa, dear Papa, often reminded us that ours was a privileged childhood. "Throughout the world," he would say, "there are thousands of people in want of shelter, clothes, and food who suffer from the cold. Remember them and don't be selfish. Thank God for being among the privileged. When you're older, help others as much as you can, and even do without a little for them."

I have never forgotten those words of wisdom. Later when life struck me hard first on the right cheek and then on the left even before I had time to turn it, Papa's advice came as a great help to me. Life sometimes takes a bad turn, you know, but no matter how bad it gets, the gift of a smile or a flower, even a wild flower, can save someone less fortunate from drowning and help us stay afloat. In the heart of every man there lies an island he can hold on to.

There was one sour note, one dark cloud hanging over the winter of my dear Grosse Ile. It was a cloud that we privileged children, engrossed in our games and our dreams about the coming Christmas, were not aware of: the loneliness the adults felt when the two ships, along with the doctors and the summer employees, had left. Isolated in the middle of the great river, six miles from the mainland, and surrounded by drifting ice floes, they were gripped by feelings of uneasiness, dread, and anxiety during the great storms when the snow filled the sky. They never admitted it openly, however, and it was only much later that I understood.

It was trying for the women to see the men leave for Montmagny to fetch the mail. They worried over their safety and must have wondered, "Will I be widowed and my children made orphans before tonight?"

Even on fair days, it was no small feat to row six miles amidst the ice floes, in the swift current, with the temperature ten, fifteen, or sometimes twenty degrees below zero Fahrenheit. Time and again, the weather was fair when they left in the morning, but then suddenly, during the trip, the wind would pick up and snow would begin to fall, impairing visibility. In winter, it was already rather dark on the river by three p.m. But St. Raphael was watching over the boatmen, and there never were any accidents.

Once, in 1910, the canoe and its crew were swept along by the river on the way back from Montmagny. The men were unable to steer it because of the tide and the wind. Darkness had fallen on the river leaving the men entirely at the mercy of the elements. They fought valiantly, relying on their instincts and praying God to reach land — anywhere. Finally, around one o'clock in the morning, the men, all but frozen, landed on the south shore upstream from Montmagny. After hauling their canoe to safety, they set out on foot and came upon a farm. There was some light inside the house, but the occupants and their dog, fearing intruders, refused to let them in. Only after lengthy explanations and much begging did the farm people open their door.

After they had seen the boatmen, everything changed. They hastened to warm them up, dry their clothes, and comfort them with a hot meal. The boatmen spent the rest of the night in comfortable beds. The next day, after a hearty breakfast, they returned to Grosse Ile.

The farmers, however, had no means of communicating with Grosse Ile or Montmagny. Imagine what those men's wives and everyone else went through, waiting for them. I should mention, however, that it happened only once in my day. Just imagine what dreadful fears the wives must have felt during every crossing.

The ice canoe used to cross the river in winter had been built by the Lachances of Ile au Canot. They were the ancestors of the Montmagny Lachances who take part in the ice canoe race held during the Quebec Winter Carnival.

The canoe was sixteen feet long and about four feet wide. It was made of oak, with one-inch thick iron ribs and gunwales. Fitted with a sail and rudder, it was a heavy boat built to withstand the impact of the ice.

It could, on occasion, carry one or two passengers. Sometimes, a mother with a young child did go along. Even though they did not help to maneuver the canoe, what courage it took!

The Grosse Ile boatmen did go through some very trying experiences. Then again, they would occasionally use a little "antifreeze" — though not too much, so as not to lose their bearings! They were wise men, the sailors of Grosse Ile.

There were six boatmen in my day: Jos Brautigam, Johnny Masson, Pit Masson, and Messrs. Caron, Joncas, and Normand. Only five of them, however, made the crossing, so there was always a man available should someone be sick or prevented from going. As they made their way between and over the ice floes, they always had to hold on to the canoe and lean forward so it would be easier to swim if they fell overboard. These were things they just knew or had learned either instinctively or from their elders.

When they reached the shore, the men had to drag the boat far enough inland so it would not drift away. They then went to a farmhouse — the Nicoles' in my day. When they were warm and had thoroughly dried themselves around the stove, they set out for Montmagny in a carriole they hitched up themselves. So, after an incredible crossing amidst the ice floes which took from forty-five minutes to three hours depending on the condition of the river, they had to travel another two miles in a carriole.

At fifteen, Éméril started crossing the river with the boatmen during his Christmas holidays. "During the crossing," he once said to me, "you have to try not to get in the water because the cold air soon freezes your clothes stiff, and the body can only endure so much cold. Of course, you are always soaked up to your thighs, but that is bearable. Once, when I was coming back from school for the Christmas holidays, we had to use poles to cross in bitter cold weather. I was sitting astride the bow to push the ice floes away. When we reached the island, my boots and the bottom of my pants legs were as stiff as stovepipes. I had to beat my legs with an oar to make them supple again. But we were never afraid on the river; we knew it and it knew us. We treated each other with respect."

Seeing the doctors leave also caused apprehension. People could get sick during the winter, and it was difficult to go to Montmagny under the best conditions. So when a storm came which lasted several days, we had to wait. It also often happened that one or two babies were born during the winter. How the mothers must have worried, knowing medical help was so far away.

I do not understand why the government, which had done so much for our material well-being and had built nice houses and large hotels, never thought of paying a doctor to stay the winter to treat the sick and deliver the babies. Construction activity started to increase in 1911. They even built a greenhouse, and a gardener came to stay year-round. A gardener was not really needed, whereas a doctor was, even if only to deliver the babies. But women were always considered "unimportant."

St. Luke, the patron saint of Grosse Ile as well as of physicians, was watching over the islanders. From high above, he provided long-distance care, and besides, we had our faith. When worried, we shared our ills and sorrows with our pastor who gave us good advice, encouraged us, and prayed for us, his parishioners. And winter came and went without a hitch.

One of Papa's articles, published in the newspaper *Le Courrier de Montmagny*, on January 19, 1907, provides a very good description of the river crossings and the births always sure to occur in winter.

Montmagny, Le Courrier de Montmagny, *January 19, 1907, volume 24, page 4.*

Grosse Ile

On the fifth of this month, Mr. Johnny Masson came to tell me that they were expecting me on Grosse Ile and that I could no longer postpone my long-awaited, promised visit.

I had just closed my carpetbag when Father Derome, returning from Quebec, came to offer me a ride in his sleigh — or rather in Jos Nicole's sleigh, for the pastor of the Quarantine Island cannot afford one on his income.

Away we went! The weather was fair, but rather cold.

The good people in and around Montmagny know what it means to cross the St. Lawrence in midwinter. But LE COURRIER has readers all over, even in Europe, and some of them will welcome more details.

Mounted on runners, the ice canoe was aground amidst the ice floes, and to reach it, we had to walk a fair distance along a path made very rough by the snow and ice. Despite the cold wind, I was quite warm when I got into the boat.

The boatmen were in position: Jos Brautigam at the helm, Johnny Masson at the bow, and Caron, Pit Masson, and Joncas at the oars.

We pushed the boat afloat and were off. I wondered how we would reach the other side of the river and I could not help worrying at the sight of the ice floes surrounding our frail craft on every side. I was soon reassured, however, when I saw that Father Derome showed not the least sign of emotion and that our brave sailors appeared to be enjoying themselves.

When the ice was strong enough, we crossed upon it. The boatmen got off and pushed the canoe up to the next lead — good exercise no doubt, but something I did not wish to take part in. There is a time for everything, and for me, the time for such maneuvers was past. Besides, Captain Brautigam was there to keep me from doing anything foolish.

Soon we were approaching the island, and it was not without emotion that I once more saw the hospital buildings, where during the previous summer, I had seen so many immigrants who had passed through looking for the happiness they could not find in their own countries. Have their hopes been realized? I sincerely hope so.

We landed. The island was all white, and I saw little children, boys and girls, playing in the snow. In places, it came up to their waists, which seemed to delight them. Their rosy cheeks attested to their good health. In their early years still, they were becoming accustomed to cold and fatigue.

My former hostess, Mrs. Johnny Masson, was the first to welcome me. In her comfortable home, I was soon warm again. My friend Johnny handed me his tobacco tin, and I packed my pipe — I felt right at home. The neighbors also came. The island's population is not very large, and in a few minutes, I had greeted all the people of the central division: Johnny Turcotte, the chief caretaker, his son, and the wireless agent, Mr. and Mrs. Xavier Caron, Charles Lagacé and his family, Victor Bédard, his wife and children. That night I would go see the Brautigams, stopping on the way to say hello to my friend P. Masson whose wife and little girl were away in Montmagny. And that would be all. Forgive me — I was forgetting the good Mrs. Métivier, her aging father, and her children. This time, I am not forgetting anybody. Grosse Ile's colony is not very large in winter; besides the pastor and the teacher, Miss Grégoire, there are in all — if I am not mistaken — forty-eight people, men, women and children.

On Sunday, we ate the traditional Twelfth Night cake at Johnny Masson's house. Johnny Turcotte found the bean, and Mrs. X. Caron, the pea. The King and Queen received warm acclaim. His Majesty Johnny I's personal advisor made a short speech in his name, promising a wise and fatherly rule. Thus ended the New Year celebrations. The next day everyone would set to work again with renewed strength and courage.

On Monday the 7th, everyone was up early to go cut ice to finish stocking the four large icehouses. An isolated spot where the water was clear and shallow had been chosen as a field of operation. Preparing those huge 25-to-30-inch thick blocks was easier said than done, and hundreds of them were needed!

You can see that people do not lead an idle life on this huge mass of ice which is Grosse Ile in winter, but they are up to it and it is with pleasure that they perform their numerous and often difficult tasks.

On Tuesday the 8th, while the caretakers were busy shoveling the snow which had fallen during the night, I suddenly heard a shout, "A fox! A fox!" It was a young one which, not having been hunted yet, was not very shy. Two little boys armed with axes started chasing it, but like quicksilver it disappeared into the woods.

Where did that animal come from? Had it crossed the river on an ice floe, or was it the offspring of the one killed last year by young Jos Turcotte? That evening I learned that two foxes had been seen. The guns were ready to welcome them properly.

All this was very interesting, but I would have liked to have gone home. Unfortunately, there was no way the journey could be undertaken. First a snowstorm, then fog caused or became the excuse for my enforced but nonetheless very pleasant stay.

On Wednesday the 9th, I went to the lower section to visit my chief and friend, Mr. Brautigam, and his large family. The man of the house was out, but I soon found him on the river, busy with his saw, ax, and crowbar. The biting wind chilled me to the bone, poor, useless spectator that I was, but he and his companions had no trouble keeping warm; the ice blocks they were lining up must have weighed at least 300 pounds apiece and moving them was far from easy.

At noon, Mr. Brautigam took me to his house for lunch. While we were smoking our pipes, waiting for the meal to be ready, Mrs. Wade [1] shouted to us that the fox was scratching the snow in front of the stable door. Mr. Brautigam quickly got his gun, but not liking this new turn of events, the fox disappeared with wondrous speed. I can tell you it would have taken a miracle to catch it.

In the afternoon, the ice cutting continued.

On Thursday the 10th, the central icehouse was almost filled up. It was exceedingly cold, and I was an unwilling Crusoe.

On Friday the 11th, same work. In the evening, all the families gathered in the schoolroom and yours truly gave a familiar, short lecture on the subject of work in a coal mine. The pastor, who had graciously agreed to preside over the meeting, ended it with some very enlightening remarks.

On Saturday the 12th, the weather was awful. It was snowing so much that we could not see twenty feet in front of us. By evening, it had become a full-blown storm. Despite the fury of the elements, Dr. Joseph Masson, of Montmagny , landed on the island. Pushed by the wind and the ice floes, his boat could not, however, reach the central division and ran ashore at the tip of the Quarantine Island. He met a group of Indians[2] on the way. He followed them and forced them to give his sister-in-law, Mrs. Johnny Masson, a beautiful baby girl. When a neighbor came too close in order to watch the Indians at their work, he was struck on the leg with a stick, which cured him of his curiosity. [3]

On Sunday the 13th, the weather had cleared. I was finally able to go home to my little family, who were beginning to get seriously worried. [4]

I thank each and every one of my Grosse Ile friends for their hospitality and invite them to visit me whenever their duties call them to Montmagny during the present winter. They will always be welcomed.

G. Vekeman

---

1 Mrs. Wade was Mrs. Brautigam's mother.
2 In Quebec, in the old days, babies were not delivered by the stork, the Indians brought them! Papa's sentence simply means that Dr. Masson came to deliver his sister-in-law's baby and that it was a girl (Géraldine).
3 Grandfather Édouard lived with his son Johnny. During the delivery, he went out for some fresh air. It was in the evening. He saw someone peering through the window, watching the said Indians give the baby to Mrs. Johnny Masson. Grandfather chased the curious intruder away with his cane.
4 Papa did not return to Montmagny with the boatmen when they went to fetch the doctor because they did not want to endanger his life because of the storm.

Everyone was ready to face the long winter.

CHRISTMAS

THE HOLIDAY SEASON

WINTER DISTRACTIONS

Materially, everyone was ready to face the long winter. But people on Grosse Ile were also concerned about their spiritual well-being. The more people felt alone and isolated, the more they felt the need to rely on some protection, some effective and unfailing support. This support we found in the simple, sincere, unwavering faith of yore. During Advent, together with our pastor — a good man, so dedicated and close to his parishioners — we prepared ourselves for the Christmas celebration. Every morning, the priest celebrated a Mass which most of the men attended. In winter, their work schedule was a lot more flexible.

In the evenings, fathers and mothers took turns looking after the children during the prayers held in our small chapel, which was heated by a big two-step stove and lit by two oil lamps. It was comfortable and heart-warming to pray in the semidarkness. It seemed to me that I heard the rustle of wings and faint echoes of "Gloria in Excelsis Deo" in the murmur of the wind!

I can still picture that small, unadorned chapel with its white walls. We were so close to the altar, just like small children come to wish their parents good night before going to bed.

Those four weeks of material and spiritual preparations made people feel good again. We were no longer alone. We felt that we were in God's hands.

Oh! the Christmases and the winters of my childhood!

Sole masters on the island under God, almost born like fish to the water, the men raised on Grosse Ile (the Massons, Brautigams, and Normands) felt at home on the river. They had mastered the art of navigation. The wives knew that, and during Advent, their confidence was restored. "The Virgin Mary was alone," mothers must have said to themselves, "and she managed to give birth to little Jesus without any help in the stable of Bethlehem. That place was less comfortable than our warm houses. She'll understand us and watch over us and our children."

Advent was a time of retreat of sorts, when people took stock of their spiritual situation after a season made eventful by numerous activities and the comings and goings of the immigrants and the summer employees. The latter could change from one year to the next. Sometimes, we got the "fox-in-the-henhouse" type. During Advent, our friendly harmony was restored. Then came Christmas, feast of all feasts, a celebration of Life, Family, and Hope.

The first midnight Mass with singing was celebrated in 1911. The schoolteacher, my aunt Eugénie Rousseau — Mother's sister — had made the children rehearse various carols. My brother Octave sang *Nouvelle Agréable*, Octave Hamel sang "Adeste Fideles," I sang "Angels We Have Heard on High," and so forth. No High Mass in Latin that year. Singing in Latin was too much to ask from our young talents. We would have been at a loss for words! Your father Éméril and his brother Henri served Mass.

After Mass, we would return home to find our presents. Such delight and such wonders! When we were little, we were not spoiled the way children are nowadays. We did not get huge piles of packages, but rather one big gift — something nice — with a few, less important packages. Strangely, each year we received exactly what we had been wishing for. The angels had guessed right!

There were also some very beautiful things in those days. Very pretty, wonderful dolls — nothing like today's ugly "Barbies." Dinner sets, sewing boxes with thread, scissors, needles, and thimbles, cribs, little sewing machines which really sewed, small windup trains, carpenter's toolboxes containing enough tools to work with, coloring books, crayons, coloring pencils, and more. And we each had a Christmas stocking filled with almonds and sweets. We kept our most treasured toys from one year to the next, and when we the Vekemans left the island, we gave a boxful of them to the little neighbors.

After marvelling at the sight of so many beautiful things, we ate a light meal, and then young and old were off to bed, for we were tired. Only later, when we were older, did we have a midnight supper. We lingered in bed the next morning, then ate a brunch. What a feast!

On Christmas Eve, as a sort of fasting, Papa did not allow us to eat any sweets. In the Christmas tree, however, besides our stockings full of treats, there was for each of us a "doughnut with a hole" hanging on a ribbon and bearing our name. It was our doughnut and no one else's, and we kept it for several days before tasting it — how delicious it was! It was a celestial doughnut brought down directly from Heaven by the Angels!

In the afternoon, we and the neighboring children showed one another our presents. In the evening, all the islanders gathered at the school to attend the pageant organized by the students.

Each year, the boys would cut down fir trees and set them up in one corner of the schoolroom. Then we would put the teacher's desk in front of them. We would cover it with heavy, grey paper to imitate rocks. On a little bed of hay, we would lay a wax figure of the infant Jesus. A big gold paper star over the crèche, icicles, smaller stars, and multicolored Christmas ornaments in the trees made the setting complete. It was wonderful!

One scene had particularly impressed me. One year, we were portraying the shepherds. The school children were dressed up in collarets and scarves to look the part. In one hand, we held a long stick made to look like a crook, and in the other, a gift the teacher had bought — our present to the infant Jesus.

In days of old, a carol was sung to the tune of *C'est notre grand-père Noé*. For the pageant, Mother had written a verse for each child. Mine went like this:

> Let us bring all our presents
> To Jesus, sweet brother
> Our young hearts, our innocence
> Are those he will prefer
> You, Jeannette, a lamb will bring
> And I with the milk shall bring
> The best round, round, round
> The best chee, chee, chee
> The best round
> The best chee
> The best round of white cheese
> To be found around here

We slowly walked up to the crèche, then knelt to lay our presents before the infant Jesus. Meanwhile the teacher quickly put out the lamps and lit a Bengal light behind us. We seemed to be blue, pink, and so on, standing amidst a blaze of light — just picture it! That, my dear children, came close to heaven. I am convinced — even to this day!— that the angels did not sing better than we did.

Then came the "You, Jeannette, a lamb will bring" verse. There was a beautiful little lamb, about six inches high, made of nice, curly wool, with a small golden bell hanging from a blue ribbon tied around its neck. I thought that lamb was so beautiful, I nearly adored it. I was the one who offered it and laid it before the crèche.

Once the pageant was over, before the people left the school, the teacher — my aunt — picked up the little lamb and said, "This lamb is yours, Jeannette."

"But it's for Jesus," I said.

"For the pageant, yes. But it is really meant for you."

Then I nearly choked with emotion. I think that is when I began having fainting fits! I was so happy to own that little sheep — so very happy, dear children, I think what grand prize lottery winners feel does not even come close.

That goes to show how simple happiness is. Oh, how things touched us! How easily we could marvel at them! And how fervently we prayed — come to think of it!

How fast time goes by. Enjoy your childhood, you, my grandchildren. Live it full of joy, wonder, and candor. The happy days of childhood are never, ever to be forgotten, especially for those lucky enough to have good parents — as you do.

Your parents may seem strict at times, but it is only because they love you. Someday you will be thankful for all their reprimands and for the straight and narrow way they helped you find amidst the twists and turns of life.

What made Éméril and me so happy on Grosse Ile was having good parents who showed us the right way. That has never worked against us.

Christmas 1911, in particular, lingers in my memory. Mother, Léon, and I sang a special carol. It was a Flemish Christmas carol whose words and music had been written by Papa's uncle, Charles-Louis Vekeman, probably sometime between 1835 and 1850.

Papa often sang that carol and had translated it into French. Mother had secretly put it into verse. She had taught it to us, and we had surprised Papa with it during the Christmas celebration at the school. I remember it as if it were yesterday. I still hear Mother's beautiful voice mingled with ours. I could see the joy in Papa's eyes; we were happy. The real magic of Christmas far surpassed our childhood dreams.

I could never find the music of that song again. As I still remember the melody, Daniel Roberge, a kind, bearded musician from St. Foy wrote down the music for me for Christmas 1980. Thank you, Daniel!

On the mountains, green and grassy
Was many a flock grazing
And scattered through the country
There were some shepherds watching
On that one night was a star
Oh! splendor shining so bright
In the sky so clear and calm
Over them casting its light   } bis

Living so close to nature
Those simple primitive men
While searching for good pastures
Were religious, musing men
The Christian faith's seed planted
In their hearts softly murmured
The foreseen times are now ended
Is he coming, our Savior?   } bis

All at once thousands of fires
Suddenly lit up the sky
And then sweet songs could be heard
All around in the still night
Filled at once with joy and fright
The excited men did see
From the sky so clear alight
The Lord's angels in glory   } bis

"Be not afraid, ye hearts faithful,"
Said the holy messengers,
"For tidings most wonderful
On this night we bring hither
He, the hope of your fathers
To drive all your woes away
And fulfill the world's desires   } bis
Was born to you on this day.

"Ye shall find Him, good shepherds,
In swaddling clothes wrapped snugly
By Mary, His sweet mother
In a stable laid gently
On the hay in a manger
Go ye now to see this King,
Long-awaited Redeemer,   } bis
Favors shall ye have from him."

Two thousand years already
Will have soon since then gone by
The good news to all revealed
Of this most wonderful night
Where'er the sun is shining
Its light on the universe
Filled with love man's adoring   } bis
He who is the world's Savior

The day after Christmas, unless it fell on a Saturday, we would go back to school. We were on holiday only from New Year's Day to January 8.

On New Year's Day, we would get up and ask for Papa's blessing. After he had passed away, Mother took over. On that day, only the oldest children went to church with their fathers. After the service, we visited all the neighbors, wishing everyone a Happy New Year. The boys pulled a sled on which stood a large bag, often a pillowcase because it did not tear like paper. At every house, we received apples, oranges, almonds, and assorted sweets. It was like Halloween nowadays.

Just like squirrels, we gathered snack food for part of the winter. Wise as always, Papa and Mother kept a discreet watch over us. They did not let us make ourselves sick by gobbling everything up the same day. Rather they made us see that it was better to eat less at a time so our stock would last longer. Moreover, they taught us not to be selfish but to share with the young ones who stayed home.

Epiphany, such a beautiful and magnificently celebrated feast in earlier days, was still observed at your grandfather Johnny Masson's home. Mrs. Masson prepared a huge cake with a pea and a bean, royal crowns, and sweets besides. It was mostly the children who celebrated and sang, while the adults talked amongst themselves. Papa always took a moment to tell us a story. Everyone, young and old, listened to him intently. He would tell us about the magi and then about the old European custom of leaving a slice of cake on the windowsill for the poor. Papa had us put this custom into practice in his own way.

On the island there lived a very poor family — a cook from the hospital, a widow with two handicapped children, who also looked after her old, blind father. They had been allowed to winter on the island.

Papa made us put aside some of our sweets as a treat for those children. I kept some for Simone, who had epileptic fits, and my brother Léon for Gérard, who was somewhat deaf and a little slow. How happy they were! And a strange thing happened that I did not understand at the time, our supplies never seemed to have diminished. Papa secretly refilled our stockings, replacing what we had given away. I realized that only much later, understanding at the same time the miracle of the loaves and the fishes. Those were heavenly candies, you see!

One Christmas, Papa suggested that I give Simone one of my dolls.

"You will still have three," he said.

"Which one shall I give?"

"The one you like best if you want your good deed to be truly meaningful."

Having said that, Papa looked at me long and hard.

I understood, and I did not cheat. I took the "latest born" of my dolls. Her head, arms, and legs were made of china. She wore delicate lace underwear. Her dress, coat, and sunbonnet were crocheted of white wool and tied with blue ribbons. Such a beautiful doll — I almost adored her — she had displaced my little lamb.

I caressed and admired the doll one last time, put it in a nice box, and ran to give it to Simone. I cannot begin to describe that poor little invalid's joy; you have to have known her to understand. I returned home happy, my feet never touched the ground.

"No regrets?" Papa asked me.

"Oh, no! Simone was so happy!"

I saw so much pride and confidence in the future in Papa's eyes. Today I understand. Papa, who had experienced life, had just bought me an insurance policy against all future trials and sacrifices which are unavoidable in this world.

After Epiphany, when the weather was nice, a few men would gather at one house or another to play cards on Sunday evenings or sometimes during the week. Not too many people played *quatre-sept*. The women looked after the children. Later, when some of the children were old enough to watch the others, the women joined in. And later still, the youths also played cards — *Euréka Joker*. We would organize a contest. There would be a grand prize, consolation prizes for everyone, and a light lunch.

Then came Shrove Tuesday. The youngsters put on disguises and ran from house to house. But from Ash Wednesday on, people stayed home. The women took this opportunity to sew for the coming summer, crochet rugs, cut rags to make rag carpets, knit, and read. As for the men, they had already taken advantage of the cold and the snow to cut some good ice, off the north shore between Grosse Ile and Ile Patience, for the icehouses.

Those were huge blocks of solid, translucent ice with glints of blue. The men bored a hole in the ice with a big auger, then used an ice saw to cut the ice blocks which were loaded on sleighs and taken to the icehouses by Pit Masson, the carter, and his assistant. In the fall, the men had removed the old sawdust from the icehouses, and they now covered the ice with the new sawdust from the last wood-cutting bee. We each had our own compartment in those icehouses, and as far as I know, no one ever took anything which did not belong to him. People respected one another.

The ice cutting work cleared a nice path across the island, and we the children rode along it on sleds, proud as peacocks. No other path was kept open in winter, so after a storm, we had to walk to school in waist-high snow. But it was quite a lot of fun for us.

Every couple in every house enjoyed a warm family life. Winter tightened family ties. Fathers could spend more time with their families.

And that is how Grosse Ile spent the winter, snugly wrapped in its white blanket of snow. We did not hibernate as bears do, but we did slow down somewhat, living without haste, peacefully, healthily. We relaxed with our families in a happy, friendly atmosphere until we heard the bell which heralded Easter and the return of spring.

Does this convince you that life on Grosse Ile in my day was not dull, even in winter, far from the outside world? The people of Grosse Ile found enough resources within themselves to lead productive, full lives and to live in harmony. Were they not wise indeed?

SCHOOL

When I first arrived on Grosse Ile, classes were held in a room of the central row. As the number of employees grew, so did the number of students. The room then became too small, and people saw fit to build a new school. And what a beautiful, roomy school it was! During our visit in 1974, one of my sons-in-law, François, was stunned to see a school so much ahead of its time and so well preserved. He thought it was wonderful; a school brightened by large windows with a dreamlike view over the river. It had individual desks, large blackboards, water closets, and sinks with running water! It was well ahead of the *Belle Province*'s country schools of the time.

Adjoining the school was a well-heated annex for our coats and boots. The teacher's lodgings comprised a kitchen, a sitting room, a bedroom, a bathroom, and a water closet. It was not one of those shabby schoolhouses one often saw in the country in those days and even much later.

From the time the summer employees arrived until the end of November, there were about forty students. Classes were given in French. There were only two or three English-speaking children and they understood French. After the summer employees had left, only about fifteen of us remained for the next four months. We were privileged then, it was like having a tutor. The teacher could spend more time with each of us. She made a point of explaining everything thoroughly: history, geography, sciences, etc. Without having to leave the island, I was able to pursue my studies, reaching the Normal School level — without, however, getting a diploma. I was taught by my aunt, who was well qualified to do so.

Even during those periods when our group was quite large, the quality of Auntie's teaching never faltered — far from it. She had more than one trick up her sleeve to get the children's attention and capture their interest.

After Miss Grégoire had left, discipline became quite lax. Come recess, we would rush outside all at once. The big boys shoved the little ones aside and tripped the girls. "Now, this is not the way for school children to behave," Aunt Eugénie said when she took over the school.

She taught us to walk out of the school like civilized children. We then went to the playground — the battery ground, where the cannons were — singing and beating time. We spent recess playing games and doing exercises. The islanders were shocked at first; they were not used to that. Johnny Masson came to my aunt's defense.

"We have never had such a capable teacher," he said. "Our children are learning a lot, enjoying school, and behaving well."

To those exercises, Auntie added round dances. The songs which accompanied them were always meant to teach us something while we played. This one, for instance: we started the round with three people, and one at a time, the others joined in while singing a verse:

> It's me who is the rose
> My name is my color
> In sweet, sweet spring I rose
> The Queen of all flowers.

Those in the round then sang:

> Come, come you charming thing
> In our games join us
> Come flower sweet-smelling
> Come, come and dance with us.

Then it was the boys' turn; they always portrayed weeds!

> Though I look like parsley
> Hemlock am I really
> Beware those that pick me
> My poison is deadly!

And the chorus answered:

> Away, away villain
> Far, far away from us
> You're so mean, you villain
> You can't come dance with us!

In addition to being ahead of her time, was Auntie a feminist? She taught us discipline, without either lecturing or punishing us. We were happy. In my day, we liked going to school.

Besides the annual Christmas pageant, Auntie always organized a big award presentation at the end of the school year. The children received their rewards from the local dignitaries: the pastor, the superintendent, the school commissioners, and the president (Papa). It was a solemn occasion. We got many prizes and medals. We left with armfuls of beautiful gilt-edged books with red bindings.

One year, Auntie also organized a picnic on the island, with games, songs, a treasure hunt, and more. It was an end-of-the-school-year reward for the children. All the parents had been invited and had contributed something to the lunch. Dr. and Mrs. Martineau joined in. It turned out to be a pleasant and successful gathering.

In 1910, Quebec-County's Legislative Assembly member, Mr. Cyrille Delage, came to the island for a visit. He spent a morning at the school, questioning the students. It was a rapid-fire series of questions and answers. He was very impressed by our school and our answers. He asked the teacher if she wanted anything for the school. "Yes. I would like a good map of Canada and another of Quebec. We only have a map of the world. It is good for the children to have a general view of all countries, but I believe they should study their country and province, Canada and Quebec, more closely." A few days after that visit, the maps the teacher had asked for arrived at the school. And did we ever study them! We were so eager, it was not long before we knew Canada "A mari usque ad mare!"

Papa, with the help of the Catholic mission, had organized a library at the school. It offered novels, biographies, accounts of saints' lives, cookbooks, handicraft books, history and geography textbooks — enough to please people of all ages. In the summer, people did not read much. But in winter, mothers would have their children ask the teacher for some book or other, and since my aunt knew everyone on the island, she would send the book most likely to please. This helped to while away the long winter evenings and increased the knowledge of one and all.

One year, a group of medical students from Laval University came to spend a day on Grosse Ile. Since the island was a quarantine station, it was only fitting that medical students should visit it and its hospital. The *Alice* had made the trip especially for them. I think there were about eighty of them in all. They were all very nice. Years ago, university students were thought to be wild. It was not true; certainly not all of them were. Anyhow they toured the island and particularly the hospital, but that was only part of their reason for coming.

When we left the school at noon, the medical students were waiting for us. They asked us all sorts of questions. We were not very old at the time. Éméril and I were ten and a half. The university students tried to stump us on many a subject, including these:

"There is a conclave in Quebec right now."

"It's not a conclave," we answered. "It's a council, a meeting of bishops. Conclaves are held in Rome when the cardinals meet to elect a pope."

"The pope lives in Quebec," they countered.

"No," we replied. "There isn't even a cardinal in Quebec right now, only Archbishop Nazaire Bégin." (He was appointed cardinal only later, on May 25, 1914.)

"The pope came to the Eucharistic Congress in Montreal," they said then.

"No," we replied confidently, "it was the nuncio, His Eminence Cardinal Merry Del Val."

We thus answered all their trick questions. They could not believe how well informed we were for people who lived on an island isolated from the world.

"Your teacher must be very nice and intelligent to teach you so many things," one of them said.

Eleven and a half year old Henri Masson replied, "Yes, and she is young and pretty, with curly blond hair and blue eyes."

At that, the students left us at once and ran to the school. There they found a teacher who was indeed very nice, but a far cry from Henry's pretty blond thing. Aunt Eugénie (the teacher) was a spinster with smooth hair pulled back in a severe-looking bun, wearing a long black dress just as severe looking. The students behaved charmingly and congratulated Auntie on the education she gave her pupils. Henri had a good laugh over the joke he had played on the medical students.

In my day, one could complete grade nine on the island. Those who wished to pursue further studies had to do so elsewhere. The students always did well upon entering colleges, convent-boarding schools, or other schools. Several went on to university. Some of my schoolmates later became priests, notaries, telegraphers, nuns, bachelors of arts, and journalists.

The education we received must not have been all that bad, for every time the inspector came, he had nothing but good things to say.

From left to right, Johnny Masson's children Armand, Arthur, Marinette, Éméril, and Henri.

What a school, my friends!

THE IMMIGRANTS

To accommodate sick immigrants, the quarantine station boasted a hospital with about a hundred beds and a clinic hotel with about forty places. The latter bore the strange name of "No. 4," probably because of its four divisions or maybe because it was one of the four old buildings dating back to the early days of the quarantine station which had not been destroyed or torn down. This hotel is still standing today.

All sick people were treated at the hospital, unless they had smallpox. Smallpox patients, which we the children used to call *picotés* (smallpoxed), were cared for in a large room of the "No. 4" hotel. That entire room was painted red, windowpanes included. In the old days, it was believed that the color red helped cure smallpox patients. Furthermore, bright light was judged harmful, hence the painted windows. The other rooms served for those who had been in contact with them.

Whenever a ship reached Pointe-au-Père, downriver, word was sent to Bic, and then, to Grosse Ile by wireless. The *Polana* gave five whistle blasts — three long and two short — to warn the hospital, when the approaching ship had finally passed Ile aux Grues.

The *Polana*, which was always on standby, would then leave with a doctor on board — in my day, it was Dr. Heylen, one of the assistants — to inspect the ship and its passengers. All diseases had to be diagnosed and treated to prevent the outbreak of an epidemic in the country.

By then, traveling conditions aboard the immigrant ships had improved. A doctor often accompanied the passengers. Later on, all immigrants were examined before sailing for Canada and the sick were turned away. Once those who had to stay on Grosse Ile had been identified, they all got on board the *Polana* and headed for the lower wharf, where Pit Masson was waiting for them with the ambulance.

Built in 1847, the "No. 4" served in my day as a smallpox hospital.

I remember those trips the ambulance made from the lower wharf to the hospital. As he drove, Pit Masson rang a bell with his foot to let the hospital staff know that he was bringing in some patients. Sometimes there were real emergencies. The ambulance was an old, closed wagon, made of wood painted black, drawn by a horse. In it were two benches mounted along each side, so the ambulance could carry two patients on stretchers. When the people were not seriously ill, the ambulance could carry about fifteen of them, sitting or standing.

All the personal effects of the newcomers had to be disinfected. Trunks, suitcases, and bundles were taken to a big shed, and decontaminated with sulphur. Likewise, the crew of the *Alice* went out to disinfect the ship which had dropped anchor off the island. This was mandatory if pestilence had been detected on board. It sometimes took two days to complete the work.

When the immigrants were cured, the steamer *Alice* took them to Quebec. They paid nothing for their passage, nor for their forced stay at the quarantine station.

Few immigrants died on Grosse Ile in my day. I do not remember any adults being buried, only children — amongst them, a very young Russian child whose relatives and friends (they were under observation at the hospital) came to the cemetery. The eldest member of the group carried the little coffin. The men stood on one side of the grave, and the women, on the other. The one who appeared to be the leader recited prayers — unintelligible to us — then lowered the little coffin into the grave. Before covering it with dirt, they hugged one other. There is a lesson to be learned from that fraternal gesture; the Russians reciting prayers in their language and we in ours, in sympathy, even though we could not understand one another.

The immigrants' cemetery in the lower section

The ambulance, driven by Pit Masson, was a closed, horse drawn wagon made of wood painted black. It could carry two patients on stretchers or about fifteen people sitting or standing.

The ambulance shed stood at the end of Johnny Masson's garden, facing the lower wharf.

Mr. G. Bilodeau, the engineer in charge of disinfection, in front of the laundry disinfecting apparatus.

The disinfection sheds

Amongst the newcomers we encountered many Germans, Flemings, Belgians, Dutchmen, Russians, Doukhobors, Galicians, Norwegians, Swedes, Frenchmen, and Swiss. Many of these people were heading for the West. The great wave of Irish immigrants had come after the famine which had plagued Ireland in 1845 and 1846.

Oftentimes, one or two members of a family would settle in Canada. Once their land or business was doing well, they would send for the rest of their families. Two Breton brothers had settled that way in the West. One day, one of them went back to get their two families. He returned with his wife, his sister-in-law, and their fifteen children. The girls all wore dresses with long waists and bodices fastened all the way to the skirt by tiny buttons in the back. The boys wore velvet pants and embroidered vests like those worn by Théodore Botrel, a French singer popular at the turn of the century.

A Swiss family also made an impression on us. Their name was Delaquis. The children, Paul and Simone, who were about my age, often came to chat with us. The immigrants could not leave the hospital grounds, which were fenced in. The "No. 4" was built next to the lower row where we lived, so now and then, we were able to make friends with some of the immigrants. The Delaquis spoke French with a pleasing accent and were quite learned. They were really nice people.

The newcomers to the country were not savages. Some of them were well-educated and quite learned. Nor did they always land on the island in large groups. Sometimes there were no more than fifteen people; now and then, only four or five had to stay at the hospital.

One day, however, before the two hotels were built near the upper wharf in 1912, two hundred and forty passengers landed on Grosse Ile. They were Doukhobors and Galicians, burly men and women, fearless people who knew all about suffering.

The first night, as there was only the "No. 4" to accommodate them, they settled in as best they could. The next day, things got better organized. The women and the children stayed at the "No. 4." The sick were already at the hospital. The *Alice* made several trips to bring food, tents, and lumber to the island. Grosse Ile's carpenters rapidly built platforms for the tents in which the men were to stay. Johnny Masson baked all night so there would be plenty of bread for everyone. The cooks also set to work.

On the evening of their arrival, when Mr. Hamel and Mr. Gamache brought the two hundred and forty immigrants their first meal, the men in the group welcomed them by kicking the trays, sending tea, sugar, bread, and everything else flying.

Mr. Hamel and Mr. Gamache ran to fetch Papa, who was busy at the hospital.

"Mr. Vekeman, " they said, "come quick. They want to kill us."

"Let's not panic," Papa said, cool and calm as usual.

Papa understood the European way of thinking, for he was himself a European. He put on his cap and walked over to the group. He was over six feet tall, weighed two hundred and fifty pounds, and had square shoulders. He was big enough not to be intimidated, even by the giant Doukhobors. He gave them the military salute, and everyone immediately fell silent. The sight of the gold braid on his sleeves and cap and of his hair and long white beard which made him look like a patriarch kept them in awe.

Papa explained the situation to them. He reminded them that they were not held prisoner but were only temporarily detained because of their sick comrades and that the latter were being treated by good doctors.

"I vouch for your safety. Don't behave like savages; show some respect and we will repay you in kind. The islanders will work all night — without getting paid extra — to ensure your well-being. We will do our best to find some food to replace that which you have scattered to the wind. Eat it, you will thus keep your strength."

The next day, Papa went to see Dr. Martineau:

"Those men are perfectly fit, " he said to him, "and with too much time on their hands, they will become troublesome, believe me. If you agree, we will lend them axes and have them clear the land behind the hospital. As a reward, I will give them clay pipes. In the evenings after supper, they can come to my place to smoke and chat with me."

"Those men could be dangerous if we give them axes," the superintendent answered, "and we have only two constables on the island. Smoking on the job is also forbidden; suppose a few of them hid tobacco to smoke during the day. Think of the fire hazard."

"Don't worry about that," Papa said. "They won't smoke on the job. I will trust them and they won't let me down. I assure you that not one of these men will try to cheat. They won't leave my garden with matches or tobacco; I take full responsibility for that. We will avoid a lot of trouble. You must understand these people. They have suffered. They fled to Canada, looking for a country where they could live in peace, and as soon as they arrived, they were submitted to checks and confined on an island. During the night, they kicked around in protest, doing some damage to the 'No. 4.' Several windows are broken."

"I trust your judgement, Mr. Vekeman, so go ahead."

It is true that we had to abide by strict rules on the island. They were necessary, for the immigrants as well as the islanders. Imagine the confusion if everyone did as he pleased!

Papa knew that it was sometimes necessary to bend the rules. He had traveled extensively, especially in Europe. He knew the people of those countries well. I think Dr. Martineau was aware of that and asked for Papa's help under such circumstances. Although people were not always aware of it, I have often seen Papa assume the role of a wise man, a true Solomon.

As predicted, the men were only too happy to work. We even had to hold them back, otherwise they would have chopped down every tree on the island. And in the evening, I well remember, they gathered around Papa who handed out pipes and tobacco. I remember the scene so vividly, I can tell you it was Carillon tobacco!

Papa would discuss one subject or other, and the men would relax and join in the conversation. As for Mother, she handed out candies to the women and children, and not knowing their language, simply smiled at them. That time, by the way, it was Papa who paid for the small treats given to the immigrants.

Their quarantine over, the Doukhobors left the island. The women got down on their knees and kissed the hem of Mother's skirt, while the men thanked Papa and kissed his hands. That scene left a deep impression on me.

There was also the mysterious story of the Russian we had nicknamed "Typhus." One day, in the fall of 1911 or 1912, word was sent to the hospital that a Russian seriously ill with typhus was to be landed on the island and that a room should be prepared to isolate him. I remember Papa telling the hospital staff that it was not a room, but rather a stretcher and a coffin that they should get ready if he was as sick as they said. The ambulance arrived at the hospital. "Typhus" got down by himself, on his own two feet, and he spent the winter at the hospital **no sicker that we were!**

It is a strange story. Papa always thought that he was a political refugee. One thing is certain, "Typhus" was not sick since not one doctor nor nurse stayed behind to look after him. Nor was he a dangerous criminal, otherwise the authorities would have put him in a real prison. There were no constables on the island during the winter. The Russian had been put under arrest by the authorities for some unknown reason. Who or what was he running from? He never said. He looked unhappy. Papa discreetly tried to make him talk, but "Typhus" never confided in him. He never lost his patience, or got angry, or made any threats. He looked mild and resigned, hoping, it seemed, for something — but what?

He had made some graffiti on the walls of his room. Papa translated several of them, amongst which: "My God, why hast thou forsaken me?" It was no fun for him. He was a prisoner, alone in a locked room of the hospital, left without any light in the evening for fear that he might start a fire. To relieve his boredom, he had only the river, which he could see through his window, and us the Vekeman children, who walked by the hospital on our way to school. He sometimes waved at us.

Anyhow, on a routine visit to check if everything was all right, Papa and Mr. Hamel discovered that "Typhus" had escaped. An alert was given. All the men set out in pursuit of him. They caught up with him on the north side of the island. "Typhus" had crossed the river on an ice-bridge and was on the other side of Ile Patience. Just a few more steps in the dark and he would have fallen into the river. Had that happened, what a heavy responsibility for the people of Grosse Ile, for the men watching him, and for the administration. But what was the idea of leaving a prisoner — no matter how harmless — on the island for the winter to begin with? The whole story was really mysterious.

So the men brought "Typhus" back to the hospital. The door to his room was double locked, and the windows were boarded up on the outside. There was enough room left between the boards so this poor man could look at the river and watch us as we walked by.

At the end of April, when navigation was once again open, he was returned to his country. Dr. Martineau had asked Papa if he would accompany him on his journey back, and Papa had accepted. He would have taken me along to visit Belgium. I would have loved it, and Mother had agreed to it. But another man was sent, a constable I believe.

Everyone was relieved to see the prisoner leave the island, for having him made everyone uneasy, but we Vekemans saw him go with an indefinable feeling of sadness.

The hospital's mysterious prisoner sometimes waved at us.

Another time, an immigrant who had had to spend a few days in hospital under observation had been really disagreeable, complaining about the food because there was no menu to choose from and no wine served with the meals. The hospital authorities told him that he was in a hospital, not a hotel, and that meals were well balanced in a hospital. Everyone breathed a sigh of relief when that gentleman left the island. Imagine our surprise when soon after quite a few newspapers printed a defamatory letter about Grosse Ile. This letter, a copy of which was sent to the Canadian government, accused the island's authorities of incompetence. The food was unwholesome, the bread — Johnny Masson's delicious bread — was revolting, and the butter, according to that gentleman, tasted like **roux fat** (which the man had written *graisse de roue* — axle grease — instead of *graisse de roux*.)

Totally discouraged, Dr. Martineau came to see Papa.

"Mr. Vekeman, what shall we do about this pack of lies?"

"Leave it to me," Papa said, "I will soon put an end to it."

It did not take long. Papa wrote a letter of his own to the government and sent a copy of it to every newspaper the gentleman had approached. I do not remember that letter by heart, but it went something like this:

"Gentlemen, you leaders of our country. To reach such high office and govern our country, it is necessary to have good breeding, an outstanding education, and foremost, a sound judgement. I do not doubt your having all three.

"Mr. X, an immigrant who spent a few days under observation on Grosse Ile and who benefited from your good care administered by your quarantine station employees, has dared to attack the way that station is run by writing a letter of condemnation.

"Knowing that you are intelligent men, I will let you — and the newspaper readers — decide whom to believe: him or the employees of Grosse Ile.

"Mr. X said, amongst other things, that our butter tasted like *graisse de roue*. To know what the latter tastes like, he must have eaten some — *we never have!*"

That put an end to it. The medical superintendent never received any letter of reprimand following the man's accusations, and he thanked Papa for his letter.

Those were neither heroic deeds nor major events in the history of Grosse Ile, but they were nonetheless some of the everyday occurrences history is made of.

I assure you that respect, dedication from non-union workers, and pride in a job well done prevailed on the island in my day. The immigrants were always well treated and well cared for at the Grosse Ile quarantine station.

The quarantine hospital in 1911. The executive staff before the hospital entrance: Nurse Beaudry, Gustave Vekeman, interpreter, Dr. Martineau, the station superintendent, and Jos Brautigam, the hosptal superintendent.

A letter written by Dr. Martineau in 1902 will give you a good idea of the things I am talking about.

Grosse Isle, Quebec, November 1, 1902.

To the Honourable
The Minister of Agriculture

SIR, — I have the honour to submit my annual report of the St. Lawrence Quarantine Service to October 31, 1902.
There were 388 vessels inspected at this station during the quarantine year, being a decrease of nineteen as compared with last year. Of these twenty-seven were sailing vessels.
The total number of persons examined was 53,379, being an increase of 13,108 over last year. These were divided amongst the different classes as follows: —
First cabin, 2,604; intermediate, 5,180; steerage passengers, 25,974; crews, 17,341; cattlemen, 2,109; stowaways, 171.

Infectious disease was reported or discovered on the following vessels, named in the order of their arrival: — SS. Tunisian, Lake Simcoe, Parisian, La Canadienne, Montfort, Ionian, Jacona, Lake Megantic, Dominion, Numidian, Mongolian, Lake Manitoba, Lake Champlain, Lake Ontario, Verbena, Kastalia, *Barque* Cambria, Tiger *and* Iberian.

The diseases as reported or found were small-pox, scarlet fever, chicken-pox, measles, enteric fever and mumps.

Only one instance occurred of a person refusing vaccination, although on three other different occasions parties refused to be vaccinated by the ship's surgeons, but consented to allow the quarantine officer to do so.

The case refusing vaccination was a passenger on board SS. Dominion, *arriving May 11, 1902. He was landed for the usual period of observation.*

Small-pox. — The government SS. La Canadienne, *Commander Wakeham, left Quebec on May 3, but two days after her departure one case of small-pox having been discovered amongst one of the crew, she then came back and arrived at the station on May 6 with 34 persons on board. We presume that the disease had been contracted before sailing, at Quebec or St. Michel de Bellechasse.*

The instructions from the department being to deal with La Canadienne *like any other vessels coming from outside ports and bringing small-pox, we removed the patient to the small-pox hospital at the station and we disinfected thoroughly the vessel with steam, sulphur, formaldehyde and bichloride of mercury. All persons were vaccinated, bathed and had their effects disinfected by the usual process. No other cases having occurred they were released on the 21st of May, after a detention of fifteen days for observation. The patient having fully recovered, was discharged from the hospital at quarantine and left the station on June 28.*

SS. Ionian, *Captain Brown, sailed from Liverpool on May 13, with 86 cabin, 153 intermediate, 597 steerage passengers and 189 crew, arrived at the station on May 24 with one case of small-pox amongst the steerage passengers.*

That case had been discovered and isolated during the forenoon of the 23rd (the day previous to the arrival of the vessel at the station). He was removed to the small-pox hospital at this station.

In order to cause the least possible delay, we asked the captain to have his steamer anchored near the station, but the pilot was not willing to take that responsibility, therefore, the vessel was left in the offing, a distance of one mile from the station, and we had to go out to her with our boats to land the passengers and their baggage, which was very inconvenient and occasioned a greater delay, and on the 26th a strong easterly gale prevented us from boarding the vessel.

Acting under instructions from the department, only the steerage passengers were landed (597 in number), with 31 steerage stewards and cooks, and the vessel proceeded with all others on May 27, after having had her hospital and steerage compartments thoroughly disinfected.

Those detained having completed the period of eighteen days for observation, and no cases having occurred amongst them, were released and left the station on June 10.

The patient was discharged from the hospital and left the station on July 5.

SS. Dominion, Captain Jones, sailed from Liverpool June 5, and arrived at the station on the 14th of the same month with 42 cabin, 96 intermediate, 718 steerage passengers, 4 cattlemen and 137 crew.

On her arrival, one suspicious case having been reported by the surgeon on board, we found after careful inspection that it was small-pox; he was immediately removed from the steamer to the small-pox hospital at the station.

The case having been promptly and satisfactorily isolated, we landed, after instructions from the department, only those being in the same compartment occupied by the sick; we disinfected carefully the hospital and the forward steerage compartment and the vessel proceeded on the 15th, leaving at the station 352 passengers and 15 members of the crew for observation. All those people were released and left the station on July 1, with the exception of the patient who was discharged from the hospital and left on July 22.

This year has been a very busy one at this station, especially at the hospital, where we had up to 106 persons at the same time suffering from different diseases.

The total number of admissions at the hospital was 264.

The deaths numbered ten; one from phthisis, three from measles, and six from scarlet fever.

In accordance with the instructions from the department, we have made careful inspection of vessels coming from South American ports, on account of the existence of yellow fever at that place. Special care has also been exercised in the inspection of vessels arriving at the station without having a clean bill of health.

Quarantine Staff. — *Dr. A. Lapointe continued, during the season, the inspection of the weekly mail steamers at the Rimouski sub-station.*

I visited this advance port, and coming up from thence on the mail steamer, made a detailed inspection between Rimouski and Grosse Isle.

The staff had also to be increased since the installation of the electric light at this station.

Requirements and Improvements. — *During the detention of the SS. Ionian's passengers, many complaints having been made about the accommodation for the steerage passengers, I am happy to say here that necessary steps were immediately taken to have the necessary improvements carried out; the water and (water) closets were put into the buildings, the sheds were divided into compartments, and a good system of drainage was introduced.*

I may perhaps be permitted to add there are still many works and repairs to do, the list of which is in the hands of the Public Works Department, and I beg to hope that they will be granted and carried out during the next year.

Reserve Inspecting Steamer. — *The great deficiency continues to be that of a strong and suitable boat, as a reserve supply, disinfecting, and mail steamer and for the forwarding of the convalescents when discharged from the hospital at quarantine.*

Deep Water Wharf. — *Another deficiency is that of a deep water wharf to which infected vessels could be brought to land their passengers and effects, and alongside of which our boats could be sheltered in rough weather and seas.*

I can only repeat, as I have always done upon every possible occasion, that those two above requirements are essential, all-important, and ever-pressing needs of the St. Lawrence quarantine service.

Steam Laundrying (sic) Disinfecting Apparatus. — *One of the most important wants for the hospital is that of a steam laundrying disinfecting apparatus, so as to sterilize the contaminated linen, clothes, bedding, &c.*

New Buildings. — *Two new buildings ought also to be erected, one to be divided so as to be used for quarters for the employees. In the previous years many of our men, being unmarried, were boarding with the other employees, and we had therefore enough buildings; but now, all the employees being married people and the staff having increased we are short of lodgment (sic).*

The other one, which should be placed in the upper part of the island, could be divided so as to give an office, a surgery, a waiting room and a room to vaccinate passengers, and on the second floor we could have four rooms in which to put the passengers suffering from diseases other than the contagious ones.

I will close my report by urging upon the importance and necessity of these different requirements that I consider essential and in the interest of the station as well as of all those concerned.

All of which is respectfully submitted.

I have the honour to be, sir,
your obedient servant,

G.E. MARTINEAU, M.D.,
Medical Superintendent,
St. Lawrence Quarantine Service

Author's notes

Some of the requests Dr. Martineau made to the government were favorably received, for by 1907, when I arrived on the island, major improvements had been made:

— A row of eight houses in the upper division
— Two houses for the doctors
— A large washhouse with disinfecting apparatus
— A school and a hotel were later built
— Two bigger ships were assigned to the quarantine station to carry the islanders and the immigrants.

Dr. Martineau also mentions October 31 as the closing date of the quarantine season. By 1910, however, navigation had greatly improved. The voyage from Europe to Canada took about ten days. So occasionally there were still ships arriving come the end of October or the beginning of November. That is why the quarantine season was extended to November 25.

It even happened one year (1912) that there were still some patients on Grosse Ile at the close of the season. A doctor and a nurse stayed behind with them. Two German children — named Klein — died, one on the 10th of December and the other on the 20th. On Christmas Eve, the icebreaker came to take the cured immigrants, the doctor, and the nurse to Quebec.

On August 15, 1909, over 7,000 Irish Canadians and French Canadians came to the Quarantine Island to pay tribute to their departed brothers. An excited, wonder-struck, nine-and-a-half-year-old girl attended the consecration of this monument.

THE IRISH MONUMENT

The remains of over 5,000 Irish lie buried under the luxuriant vegetation of Grosse Ile. Blanketed in green, the emblem of Ireland and the color of hope, the island gently rocks them and offers a hope of peace.

In 1909, a monument was erected on the island in memory of the Irish. It was quite an emotional event for us because the plight of the Irish immigrants had become part of the history of the quarantine station. I was only nine and a half at the time, but my memories have not faded.

Returning from the hospital one evening, Papa told us that Fallon Bros. of Cornwall (Ontario) had been awarded the contract for the monument and that its base would be made of granite from the quarries of Stanstead (Quebec). That name had fascinated me then, and coincidentally, many years later, Éméril and I lived in Stanstead.

It was the Ancient Order of Hibernians which realized the wish of many to erect an Irish memorial on Grosse Ile. It donated 5,000 dollars for that purpose. A cross, about 15 feet high, was to surmount the monument whose design was intrusted to Mr. Jeremiah Gallagher. The Honorable Matthew Cummings, international president of the Order, came to Canada for the occasion. The site chosen for the monument was on the highest point of **Telegraph Hill**. The 48-foot monument, overlooking Grosse Ile and the river, would thus bear witness to the past.

On August 15, the day of the unveiling, over seven thousand Irish and hundreds of French Canadians came to pay tribute to their departed brothers. To avoid any incidents on that day, the young children living on Grosse Ile had been forbidden by the authorities to mingle with the crowd. Éméril, however, did witness the arrival of the flotilla of boats and yachts, bedecked with flags, which carried the visitors. The steamer *Alice* had the honor of bringing the official representatives of the Irish orphans adopted by Quebecers. Éméril remembered how moved those people were when they set foot on Grosse Ile.

Arrival of the visitors and dignitaries, August 15, 1909.

For some reason I escaped the interdiction and was allowed to follow Papa during the ensuing ceremonies. I remember two things clearly. Papa was holding my hand and we were both reading aloud the inscription on the monument.

"Sacred to the memory of thousands of Irish emigrants who, to preserve the Faith, suffered hunger and exile in 1847-48, and stricken with fever, ended here their sorrowful pilgrimage."

Several wreaths of flowers lay at the foot of the cross including one given by Dr. Martineau on behalf of Grosse Ile and one given by Mr. Cyrille Delage, the president of the Société Saint-Jean Baptiste de Québec. I do not recall the names of all the donors, but one arrangement made an impression on me because it was in the shape of an anchor. I thought about the Irish who had dropped anchor at Grosse Ile long ago — and it seemed that this anchor had now blossomed.

Then I see myself again, sitting on the dignitaries' platform. I had no right to be there, and a man came to take me away. To no avail. I was glued to my seat, close to tears. Standing nearby, Papa moved closer and whispered something into the man's ear. I do not know exactly what it was, but the man let me stay on the platform, picked up a flower, and gave it to me — no doubt to keep a tear from rolling down my cheek.

My young heart was overcome by the sight: the crowd kneeling and overwhelmed by emotion; the cadets of the Ancient Order of Hibernians forming an honor guard; and the Hussar band accompanying the "Libera" sung by Archbishop Bégin.

After the religious ceremony, several people made speeches: His Eminence Donatus Sbarretti, who was the Apostolic Delegate to Canada, Father Hanley, pastor of St. Patrick's in Quebec, and officials of the federal and provincial governments.

The moment which seemed the most touching to me was when Father Maguire recalled the memory of the forty-four priests who devoted themselves to the immigrants in 1847, displaying unsurpassed courage. Besides helping the doctors, the Catholic and Protestant clergymen comforted the dying in their final moments. Father Maguire paid homage especially to Father Hugh McGuirk, the last surviving priest, who, at age ninety-six, could not be present at the ceremony. He then called an elderly person to step forward, a Mrs. Roberge from Quebec, an Irish orphan taken in by a Quebec family. She represented some six hundred Irish orphans adopted in the province of Quebec.

In closing, Father Maguire mentioned the doctors who died while performing their duties on Grosse Ile in 1847. At the entrance of the Irish cemetery in the upper section, near Cholera Bay, a monument recalls their dedication.

At the end of the day, a little girl, down from her platform and overcome by emotion, thought that even though the Irish memorial on Grosse Ile recalled a painful chapter in the history of Ireland, it was also a symbol of love and friendship.

May the world one day understand.

In 1913, the islanders began to pray to the Virgin Mary and pledged to erect a statue in her honor if Antoinette were to be cured.

THE ISLAND'S STATUE

"OUR LADY OF THE ROCK"

In the spring of 1913, Dr. Martineau arrived with his family. Seriously ill, his daughter Antoinette was brought ashore on a stretcher. The doctors who had attended her during the winter had not been able to cure her.

The islanders began to pray to the Virgin Mary and pledged to erect a statue in her honor if Antoinette were to be cured. It was a miracle. To the doctors' surprise, Antoinette recovered.

On August 22 of the same year, all the islanders gathered for the consecration of the statue.

In 1979, at his request, I related to Father Sénéchal, the pastor of Ile aux Grues, the events which led to the presence of a statue of the Virgin Mary on Grosse Ile. While checking a date in the archives of the archdiocese of Quebec in late December 1980, I came across some of Mother's writings. She related what I was writing down for Father Sénéchal almost word for word. This shows that my feelings at the time did not spring simply from youthful enthusiasm, but were shared by my parents and such men as Côme Langlois — who sang the "Magnificat"— and Dr. Heylen, a Protestant, who remarked in broken French after the ceremony that the priest had really said beautiful things.

Here is what Mother wrote:

CONSECRATION OF A STATUE

With the superintendent's permission and the help of Mr. Tremblay, Mr. Beauchemin, and some workmen, our pastor was lovingly making preparations for the installation of a statue of the Immaculate Virgin. Because of the nature of the rock — which crumbles when it is cut — a niche could not be carved. So our pastor had a cement-covered, wooden frame made, with a cross surmounting its dome. This cross and the upper part of the niche are adorned with little electric bulbs which form a bright nimbus around the Virgin's head. Dressed in white with a blue belt and a silver rosary, the Madonna stands out marvelously well against the rocky grey background with shrubs and wild flowers springing from every crevice. Thirty wooden steps covered with cement lead up to the little platform on which stands the niche. They wind their way up the uneven rock face, and each of them is decorated with a pot of natural flowers or an ornamental potted plant, for the most part donated by the parishioners. A green lawn lies at the foot of the rock face which forms a natural throne. In front of the statue, there is a circular bed of flowers whose fragrant cups sway gently before the Immaculate Virgin, exhaling their heady fragrance toward Her like so many little censers, whenever there is a breeze.

On the evening of the consecration, the rocky hill and its gardens took on a kind of ethereal air, sparkling brightly from top to foot. Four long rays made up of myriad Chinese lanterns joined the four angles of the niche to two corners of the chapel on one side and two corners of the presbytery on the other. Everywhere, through the trees hanging on the face of the rock or standing on its top, we could see other lights, soft and veiled, shining like so many stars, swaying gently in the breeze.

The air was warm and still; it had threatened to rain all day. Upon meeting our pastor in the afternoon, I had asked him if he feared rain for the evening. "Oh! The Virgin will no doubt finish what she has started," he had said. "I leave her to do as she sees fit, and I am confident it will go well." He had been right to trust her: not one drop of rain fell during the open air ceremony, but just as soon as the people had returned home afterward, it began to drizzle. The rain increased gradually during the night, and the earth, thirsty after several days without rain, drank more than its fill.

The religious ceremony thus took place in the quiet atmosphere of the warm evening, on the lawn of fragrant flowers, under a myriad of lights, before the graceful, white Madonna, and in a perfect harmony of souls and hearts, united in paying tribute to Her. One voice, trembling with emotion, began to sing "Ave Maris Stella," and numerous others fervently joined in. Then Father Paré, a teacher from the Quebec Seminary and our pastor's brother, stood on the porch of the presbytery and made a rather moving speech before the crowd.

After that eloquent speech, Mr. Côme Langlois, the good captain of the Alice, *struck up the "Magnificat." This sacred hymn, born out of Mary's grateful soul, brought everyone's enthusiasm to its peak. It was a beautiful scene: the whole crowd, standing as one, joined in the chorus in perfect harmony. And while we sang the final verses, we saw the priest in his vestments, followed by the altar boy in a white surplice, slowly make his way through the greenery, the lights, and the flowers, up the thirty steps leading to the feet of the Virgin. He was going to sprinkle some holy water on the statue and to recite the prayers which would consecrate both the statue and the rock to the glory of Mary. Though we had not known it until then, it seemed that the Lord had created them expressly to serve as a pedestal for his Divine Mother.*

The two ascending shadows, sometimes partly veiled by the branches of a shrub and then suddenly emerging in full sight, seemed to want to climb to the sky. Seeing that, one naturally thought of Jacob's mysterious ladder which the Angels of God ascended and descended. Surely the Angels were also climbing the stone steps at that moment; surely they were moving about in the greenery with its fiery flowers, hovering above the fervent and contemplating crowd. Their love for their noble sovereign could not but lead them to join in such an eager, joyous, and heartfelt tribute paid to her by her earthly children.

The religious ceremony ended — too soon alas! everyone thought — with the moving French hymn "Le chant du soir à Marie" ("Evening Song to Mary") sung with the utmost piety by Father Horace Gagnon of the Quebec Seminary.

> *OH TUTELARY VIRGIN!*
> *OH YOU OUR ONE AND ONLY HOPE!*
> *TO OUR PRAYER LISTEN*
> *TO OUR EVENING PRAYER AND SONG*

How the chorus resounded! How fervently we sang! The Virgin Mary was truly a queen at that moment — loved, respected, and trusted.

To ensure that the echoes of that unforgettable celebration would ring as long as possible and that its salutary effects would last henceforth, our pastor has gotten into the delightful habit of gathering us often at the feet of our Virgin for the evening prayer accompanied by hymns. It is our public way, on the first Saturday of the month, to make amends and pay tribute to Mary Immaculate.

N.B. This text was taken from *Échos religieux de la Grosse Ile (Grosse Ile's Religious Newsletter)* and is signed Jeanne des Érables, Mother's pen name.

Public Health Branch
Department of Agriculture

Dominion Quarantine Station

Rev. E. Paré,   *September 11, 1913.*

Sir:—
The following are the only facts within my knowledge of the illness of Miss Antoinette Martineau.

As far as I know, Miss Martineau took sick in March last. Her case puzzled the physicians but I believe eventually was pronounced to be 'General Tuberculosis'. At the request of Dr. Martineau I made examinations of the sputum, urine and faeces, but was unable to detect the presence of 'Bacillus Tuberculosis'. When I first saw her in April she was simply skin and bones, and refused all food. She had not eaten since the beginning of her illness, and was troubled with vomiting which was independent of food and appeared to be nervous in origin. Her physicians thought at this time that she was suffering from Tuberculosis of the Peritoneum. Her complete refusal of all nourishment and the vomiting persisted until June (Corpus Christi) when, following the annual procession and benediction, the ostensorium containing the Host was held for a few moments over her bed. The vomiting I believe ceased and she began to eat on the following day. Subsequently she had an attack of Pneumonia with slight hemorrhages from the lungs. At present she is convalescing rapidly.

Sincerely yours
J.J. Heagerty, M.D., D.P.H.

Unabridged copy of Dr. Heagerty's letter attesting Antoinette Martineau's recovery. Mother translated this letter into French. It was published in *Échos religieux de la Grosse Ile*. This document is kept in the archives of the diocese of St. Anne de la Pocatière.

IMAGES OF MY CHILDHOOD

Images of my childhood,
Beacons of light throughout my life.

Jeannette

Dear children, I take the liberty of including a chapter about Grosse Ile's scenery. I often mention it throughout this story simply because nature in all its beauty was so magnificent that it held me under its spell.

I remember amongst other things the fall we arrived on Grosse Ile. One morning, Léon and I were talking and admiring the beauty around us on our way to school. We began to explore a little way off the path, moving from one discovery to the next until we reached the ridge near the Catholic chapel.

Numerous beautiful clusters of ripe fruit hung from the branches of the cherry trees. We ate our fill. I do not remember what Léon did next — sleep maybe? He was only six and a half. For my part, I was enraptured by my surroundings — nature, serene and bountiful. From where I stood, I saw the river moving in leisurely fashion and the sailboats gliding on its surface. White gulls flew to meet them. The smell of the sun-warmed earth, mingled with that of the weeds of September, was already that of fall. I could no longer move. Time stood still, and my heart had stopped — how beautiful the world was!

At home, however, Mother had not lost track of time. When we did not return for lunch, she came looking for us. I saw her and called, "Mother!" Her joy at finding us did not immediately erase the apprehension on her face. I promised myself never to scare her like that again.

I still recall waking up in the morning after it had snowed all night and running to the window. "Everything is thick white!" we would say, filled with wonder. We left for school, walking through the snow which nothing — not even a bird — had disturbed. For a while, Léon and I would go on alone and not dare to speak. We were afraid of breaking the spell. Our feet raised a fine, sparkling powder which looked like stardust. The island looked like a white castle. The ice floes on the river were soldiers mounting guard, protecting our castle from invaders. The trees, decked in white, bowed before us.

It was not the cold which took our breath away, but the splendor of this fairy tale come to life.

Another time — I must have been eleven years old — I was on my way to the chapel for the evening prayer. I was walking through the small wood between Pit Masson's and Johnny Masson's houses. Through the clearings, I saw the wharf and its shed, a silvery silhouette against the sky. The moon shone so bright and the snow sparkled so that I dropped to my knees saying, "My God, it's so beautiful. So beautiful!"

We did not live in the hope of some distance happiness; we were happy. How sweet our lives were.

Éméril also told me about winter evenings on the island. He and his sister Marinette often went to sit on the wharf. Both would let themselves be spellbound by the magic of the river heaving to and fro to some strange music: He, hee, cabang, cabang-crack, the sound of the water and the ice floes crashing into one another; he, hee, cabang, cabang-crack, moonlit music, he, hee, cabang, cabang-crack, played by Neptune only for them.

I often mention the tides. It is no secret that the tide always rises higher during the full moon. And there are also what we called "the great tides" every spring and fall.

During those great tides, water invaded our backyard and flowed freely between the summer kitchens and the back of our row of houses. The river licked greedily at the stilts of our kitchen.

Once, pushed by a very strong northeast wind, the great fall tide flooded the lower levels and invaded our kitchen. The whole family went up to the bedrooms above it. I was the last one to leave the kitchen; I hastily picked up a few small objects now floating on the water and put them on the table. Soon five or six inches of water covered the floor. I then joined the others who were not in the least worried. We knew that at the usual time, the tide would begin to ebb. So we succumbed to the spell of the unleashed elements, while Papa told us stories and grandmother Rousseau said her rosary in a hushed voice.

The wind howled; the raging waves carried away the wood stacked in our backyard. Huge snowballs, shaped by the moving water, passed so close to the house that we feared for the kitchen windows. I was sure I could never forget how I felt at that moment.

When the water had receded, I bored some holes in the floor with an auger to let the water run back to the river. I then plugged the holes with pegs cut from an old broomstick. Mother and I gave the walls and the floor a good scrub — and thus we did the kitchen's spring-cleaning that fall!

The next day, what a sight! All around the house were logs and snowballs frozen solid to the ground. Using an ax, we salvaged our firewood. Some immigrant women were still on the island for observation. They were staying at the "No. 4." When they saw us gathering our firewood, they came to help. Nothing could have stopped them; they were more than happy to lend a hand. They had guessed that it was our supply for the winter. As I have said before, those women were not sick, but only under observation. Theirs was a spontaneous gesture which not only warmed our hearts for that short winter spell, but which echoed through my life.

We did not always live with our heads in the clouds on Grosse Ile; usually we kept our feet firmly on the ground or in the water. We had to live with the elements. For dreamers, it was poetry and it was beautiful.

Every year, toward the end of May or the beginning of June, there appeared small, winged insects called ephemerids. They did not survive more than a day, hence their name. They looked like dragonflies — we called them mayflies.

The arrival of the mayflies was quite an event for the children. They arrived in thousands, always on a fine evening. Spring was in full bloom; nature was coming back to life. Sitting on the grass near the house, we would watch those insects all evening long; myriads of small, winged creatures waltzed in the glow of the electric lights.

One year, there were so many of them that the island employees had to gather them up in wheelbarrows and burn them. Ephemeral little insects, dead come dawn for having danced too much during the night, had you something to teach us?

I remember rainy days. We went up to the attic and there, comfortably installed on old rag carpets, we looked out of the dormer window. The river opened up to welcome the raindrops and rolled them into waves. The song of the rain falling on the roof often lulled my little brothers to sleep. And I felt so good, so happy, so much in tune with life.

110

I also remember warm summer evenings. People kept silent to hear the sounds of the night. There was the chirping of the crickets, and mysterious rustles in the grass, and the "shoo, shoo" of the generator. The lights of the lower wharf were mirrored in the river, and fireflies lit their lanterns. The night wrapped the island in sweet mildness.

I could still go on depicting such scenes for pages and pages.

> Oh, images of my childhood,
> Beacons of light throughout my life.

One of our neighbors on Grosse Ile, Octave Hamel, wrote to me in May 1980. I include his letter here as a token of our friendship for this dear man, who passed away in early 1981.

To him who has become one of our cherished memories.

Lauzon, Que. May 26, 1980

Mrs. Éméril Masson
R.R. #3, Stanstead, Que.

Dear you two,

I can't tell you, dear Jeannette, how much I enjoyed your and Isidore's visit. So many beautiful childhood memories came back to me. It made me rather sad, at the same time, not to see Éméril with you. I would have liked so much to see him again too after so many years apart — well over sixty years, for I was still very young when he left Grosse Ile to settle on a farm with his mother and the rest of his family, and I haven't seen him since. But you, Jeannette, you came to visit us once in Lauzon, at least twenty-five years ago, didn't you?

Since your visit, I have often thought about the happy days of our childhood; of our neighborly relations; of our years at the communal school so well directed by your aunt Miss Eugénie Rousseau; of your old grandmother who lived with her; of your parents Mr. and Mrs. Vekeman; of Léon; of Gustave; of beautiful Grosse Ile, every corner of which we visited and which I have always seen as a real paradise. And of your husband's family: Mr. and Mrs. Johnny Masson, Henry, Armand, Petit Jos — as we called him — Marinette, Rosa, who unfortunately died so young, and Géraldine. So many memories. Does Éméril remember our fishing trips? Our seining when we sometimes brought back miraculous catches, which allowed us to sell fish to the islanders? And our excursions to the neighboring islands to pick strawberries, raspberries, and blueberries on the fairest of days which Providence provided for us on those occasions? There's no doubt about it, we were happy together; I doubt that many people could say the same. And we could travel to either Quebec or Montmagny for free whenever we pleased.

And how could I not remember our good pastor, Father Paré, who gave us our first Communion, and confirmed us, and taught us to sing? I was truly fond of that dear pastor, and I often pray to him. But the years went by rapidly, and reluctantly we left this enchanting island which we will forever fondly remember. And I think it must be the same for you two — I am sure of it. So here, dear Jeannette, are the memories you left behind when you came to visit us. Let us hope we will be able to meet again soon.

Your old friend, Octave.

We did not live in the hope of some distant happiness; we were happy. How sweet our lives were.

So many memories!

MISCELLANY

PILGRIMAGE TO THE SHRINE OF ST. ANNE

In tribute to the government which put the *Alice* at the islanders' disposal every year for a pilgrimage to St. Anne de Beaupré.

This pilgrimage took place at the end of August or the beginning of September. We left early in the morning. On the way, our pastor said the rosary and made a few exhortations. He prompted us to trust in St. Anne's intercession. We sang hymns. Once we had reached Beaupré, it was time for confessions, a High Mass, communion, and a sermon.

At noon, we ate under an awning set up alongside the basilica and extended over some tables and benches. The mothers had packed a big lunch. For the children, it was a little like a picnic. We drank the water which flowed freely from a faucet into a basin surmounted by a statue of St. Anne. We thought of that water as an elixir of life, and as far as Éméril and I are concerned, it was!

After lunch, we toured the various holy buildings: the Scala Sancta, which we climbed on our knees, the small and very old chapel built by French sailors, and the cyclorama, a fascinating sight I remember vividly.

At two o'clock, we went back to the basilica for the remaining ceremonies: the veneration of a relic of St. Anne, the benediction of the Blessed Sacrament, a sermon, and the blessing of the souvenirs. The boys sometimes wanted to have even some pocketknives and small telescopes blessed, and the girls, some handbags and bracelets. We believed them to be holy objects since we had bought them from various stands on the sanctuary grounds! Afterward, we returned to the island.

At home, for days hence, we would play pilgrimage. Standing on a chair, my brother Léon, dressed in a nightgown, made some very convincing sermons, imitating the preachers' voices and gestures, and then blessed us. He excelled especially in the sprinkling of holy water — he did not spare it!

Our neighbors, the Hamels, had a little girl who could not walk. Her hands and feet dangled lifelessly from her limbs. Otherwise, she was very bright and vigorous. When she was four, her mother and grandmother vowed to take turns carrying her in their arms, without anyone else's help, during the day of pilgrimage, in hopes of a cure.

Before fall was over, little Germaine was playing and running about with the other children. Last spring, I talked to her on the phone. She told me her health was good, and she had never had a relapse. She must be in her seventies now.

THE PASTOR'S INTERVENTION IN TIMES OF DIFFICULTY

In January 1907, when Mrs. Johnny Masson had just given birth, Éméril seriously injured himself. Like all little boys their age, Éméril and his brother Henri liked to wrestle and jump up and down on their beds while throwing pillows at each other. One day, caught up in the excitement of the game, Éméril lost his balance and fell backwards, knocking the back of his head hard against one of the posts of his iron bedstead. He had a nasty wound and was losing a frightful amount of blood.

Someone called Father Derome who rushed right over. He succeeded in stopping the bleeding, disinfected the wound, and applied a thick dressing. He gave some advice to Miss Grégoire — the teacher — who had come to care for Éméril, which she did with all the love and dedication of a mother. Mrs. Masson was too weak to look after him, her last child being only a few hours old.

Another time, Éméril, then eleven, was helping his father free some wood from under the snow for the bread oven. In so doing, they ended up digging a tunnel under the snow. After Johnny had finished bringing in the wood, Éméril lingered behind to play in the tunnel. The snow collapsed, and Éméril was buried under it.

As it was time for school, the children said good-by to their parents and left. Éméril was not with them, so Johnny then figured out what had happened. He ran quickly to the woodpile, saw a mitten sticking out of the heap of collapsed snow. Quickly but carefully, he freed Éméril, who was unconscious.

I can still see this tiny, unadorned chapel with its white walls.

Once again, someone telephoned the pastor. Father Derome's successor, Father Paré, gave Éméril artificial respiration for a long time and rubbed him down. Éméril finally came to. After examining him, Father Paré said there were no broken bones, although Éméril's body was all covered with blood which oozed out from the pores of his skin. Éméril's eyes were also frightfully bloodshot. After three days of rest, he regained his strength. How happy we were to see him back in school. Éméril, who was liked by everyone — and not just me! — was the hero on that day.

One winter, my brother Gustave was quite ill and almost succumbed to pleurisy. He ran a high fever and was delirious. A storm had been raging for several days, so we could not see ten feet in front of the house. My brother's condition suddenly took a turn for the worse. Mr. Johnny Masson offered to try crossing the river to fetch the doctor. With an aching heart, Papa, who was fair and wise, refused to jeopardize the lives of five boatmen — all family men.

"The Lord will provide," he said.

Once more, the pastor was called in. Father Ferland, who had replaced Father Paré, made his way through the storm and spent the night with us. I stayed up too; I did not want to see that dear little brother of mine die.

The next morning, Father Ferland blessed my brother Gustave.

"Mr. Vekeman," he said, "you made the right decision about the boatmen yesterday. You acted according to your conscience. I'm leaving to go say Mass for your little sick one. Don't worry. Take heart. Your son will recover."

Father Ferland disappeared into the storm, and at the moment the service ended, Gustave's temperature came right down to normal. It took him some time to recover fully. He had been very sick and was frightfully thin, but by the next summer, he was able to join in his friends' games.

So I know of three occasions when the intervention, advice, and prayers of three different priests benefited the people of Grosse Ile simply because we had faith in God.

THE PARROT

A sailor had given Johnny Masson's children a beautiful parrot. It caused quite a stir amongst the island's children. We had seen parrots in our books, we knew they could talk, but to actually see a real one, brightly colored, alive and talking, was something fantastic worth boasting about.

There was, on the island, a rather elderly gentleman — one of the doctors — who was, in politics, a true-blue conservative. Johnny's children had taught the parrot to say, "Hello, damn Tory," and whenever the gentleman in question walked by, Arthur — the rascal of the family — had the parrot repeat this greeting. And when Mother — who was so small —

passed by, the bird would say, "Hello, po' little one, po' little one." Johnny finally got wind of those pranks and put an end to them. "You might think it's funny," he said to the children, "but you are being rude to these people."

The children understood and stopped at once, but it took the parrot a little longer!

A CRYSTAL WEDDING ANNIVERSARY
MY STROKE OF GENIUS AT AGE TWELVE

In April 1912, my parents were to celebrate their crystal wedding anniversary. I wanted to surprise them with a gift, but how? I had little money. And of course, I had to give them something made of crystal. So I got the idea of asking Johnny Masson to bring me back a big glass of mustard the next time he went to Montmagny! I had 25 cents in my piggy bank. I made him cross his heart not to tell Léon, and least of all my parents, and to deliver the said glass secretly and to no one but me. He looked at me in surprise. He and his wife looked at each other questioningly, not understanding why all the secrecy about a jar of mustard.

"Why?" they said at last.

So I explained that it was for my parents' crystal wedding anniversary.

"They like mustard a lot, and the glass, so pretty, will remain as a souvenir."

That was my stroke of genius at age twelve. Mr. and Mrs. Masson understood and rose to the occasion.

"Wait for us Sunday," Mrs. Masson said to me, "and do not give them your present before we're there."

The big day came. Sunday after supper, Mr. and Mrs. Masson arrived, each carrying a package they hid in the hall. Everyone chatted, and it was a pleasant evening. Finally, I was given the signal and got out the glass of mustard decorated with a bow of ribbon tied to its handle. Johnny fetched the two hidden packages: his package contained a beautiful platter made of real crystal on which regally lay a twisted rope of blond taffy as only Johnny could make it and which Papa just loved; in Mrs. Masson's package was a bowl — also of crystal — filled with maple cream fudge. All those sweets made my mustard less bitter! But my glass was nonetheless proudly displayed on the table. That evening, my parents were very happy and marveled at the Massons' sincere friendship and at their twelve-year-old daughter's love — and stroke of genius!

When I got married, Mother gave me the platter, the bowl, and the glass for good luck.

A CORRIDA WHEN THE TORERO RUNS AWAY!

Every spring, we fetched a young bull from Ile aux Grues for the island's herd of cows. The youths liked to tease the bull which made him mad so that it sometimes became dangerous for the little ones going to school or playing outside.

One morning, during the summer vacation, I said to Mother, "I'm taking the little ones out to pick raspberries for dessert at lunch."

"All right," she said.

So I left. My brothers and I were picking raspberries in the middle of a field where the cows were grazing, but as they were very far from us, I was not worried. Suddenly the bull spotted us. He left the herd, and snorting all the way, charged toward us. What could we do? I barely had time to sit Gustave on my shoulders, and holding Isidore by the hand, I started walking — fast. We came to a ridge of rock with a very steep path leading to its top. The bull could not climb up this path. One more minute, and it would have been all over for us.

I waited a long time. When I thought it safe, I went down the other side of the ridge with my brothers, then walked along a small clump of trees which would hide us from the animal. To my horror, the bull appeared on the other side of the clump. Had it guessed my plan? We thus came face-to-face. The bull stopped, shook its head, and watched us go. Our guardian angels must have interposed between the bull and us — there were no raspberries for dessert at lunch that day!

Another time, I was coming back from the evening prayer, and the bull was standing in my way in the small wood between the bakery and Pit Masson's house. It would have been dangerous to turn my back on the bull; it would have chased me and I would not have been able to reach a safe place in time. By some miracle, Pit Masson, who was outside, saw the whole thing from afar. "Don't be scared, Jeannette," he yelled to me, "stay calm." He came running, grabbed a plank from the boardwalk, and used it to force back the bull which was bellowing and pawing the ground. I ran as fast as I could. From that day on, Pit Masson was a hero in my eyes. Olé torero!

In summer, the arrival of the public works foreman was quite an event. It meant the construction of new buildings and the possibility of repairs or improvements to the islanders' houses.

For two years, the foreman had been a widower, a very short man whom the people called *"le petit veuf"* (the little widower). One day, Mrs. Bédard asked Mrs. Johnny Masson, in my presence, if *"le petit veuf"* had arrived. Eager to show off, I hastened to answer yes.

I had heard *"le petit boeuf"* (the little bull), and I went on, proud as a reporter returning to his newspaper office with a scoop.

"Yes, it [1] has arrived, and it is not very smart, it is tame this year. We pat it on the back and neck. We scratch it behind the ears and it doesn't move; it seems to like it."

Both women then burst out laughing. They giggled so much, and I could not fathom why.

"It's true. It's not very smart, and it likes to be patted," I repeated almost offended.

Finally understanding my mistake, Mrs. Masson came to my rescue and set things straight. After those adventures, I gave up corridas!

---

[1] In French, the same pronoun — *il* — can refer to the man and the bull.

My father strolling in the woods between Johnny's and Pit Masson's houses. On the right, the pipe which carried water to the houses and which was buried in 1913.

Édouard Masson

THE MASSON FAMILY

It is almost impossible to talk about Grosse Ile without mentioning the Massons. Four generations of them have lived there. They were good people. They have definitely left their mark on the island.

Édouard, the first of the Massons, came to the island in 1863. At one time, he acted concurrently as caretaker, baker, carter, ambulance driver, and boatman. He had nine children, amongst them Jean-Baptiste, known as Johnny, Pierre, knows as Pit, and Joseph, who all became involved with the Quarantine Island.

You will find on the following pages a table of the Massons and the Vekemans mentioned in this book. When I talk about Jean-Baptiste and Pierre Masson, I call them Johnny and Pit, not to be disrespectful but because they are remembered by those names.

Édouard MASSON m. 1864 Zoé POULIOT

1	2	3	4	5
Georges	Anna	**Jean-Baptiste** (Johnny) m. 1897 Éléonore DELORME	**Joseph** m. 1902 M.-Anne Conney	**Pierre** (Pit) m. 1905 Léa Lemieux

1. Georges-Henri	1. Wilson	1. Lucienne
2. Éméril	2. Malcolm	2. Annette
3. Marinette	3. Harold	3. Georges
4. Arthur		4. Robert
5. Armand		5. Paul-Aimé
6. Rosa		6. Lucien
7. Géraldine		7. **Freddy**
8. Marie-Jeanne		8. Gemma
9. Joseph		9. Madeleine

1	2	3
MARIE-ANTOINETTE (Jeannette) m. 1925 **ÉMÉRIL MASSON**	Léon	Jean-Joseph dec'd

1	2	3	4	5
Marie-Claire m. 1954 Clayton Enright	Jean-Baptiste m. 1956 Jacqueline Camirand	Gustave m. 1951 Gisèle Aucoin	Rose m. 1956 François Dompierre	Cécile m. 1958 Edgar Gouin

1. Martin	1. Carl	1. François	1. Dominique	1. Nelson
2. Thomas (Tommy)	2. Jean-Luc		2. Pascale	2. Véronique
3. Marie	3. Pierre		3. Julien	3. Sonia
			4. Moïra	

m. 1980
Denis Chouinard

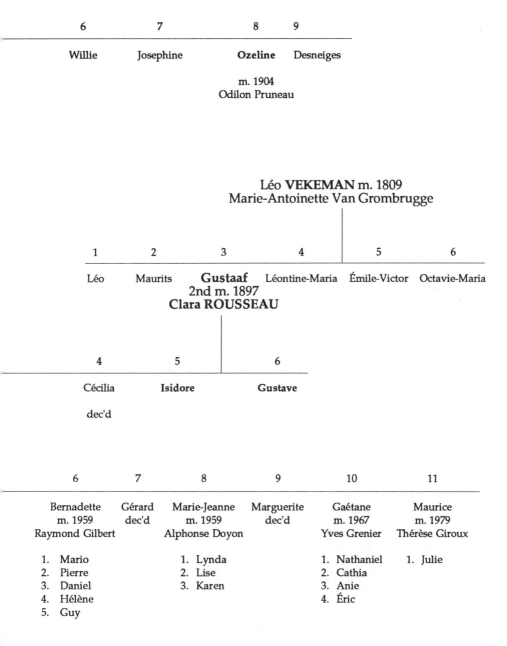

6	7	8	9
Willie	Josephine	**Ozeline**	Desneiges

m. 1904
Odilon Pruneau

Léo **VEKEMAN** m. 1809
Marie-Antoinette Van Grombrugge

1	2	3	4	5	6
Léo	Maurits	**Gustaaf**	Léontine-Maria	Émile-Victor	Octavie-Maria

2nd m. 1897
Clara ROUSSEAU

4	5	6
Cécilia	**Isidore**	Gustave
dec'd		

6	7	8	9	10	11
Bernadette	Gérard	Marie-Jeanne	Marguerite	Gaétane	Maurice
m. 1959	dec'd	m. 1959	dec'd	m. 1967	m. 1979
Raymond Gilbert		Alphonse Doyon		Yves Grenier	Thérèse Giroux
1. Mario		1. Lynda		1. Nathaniel	1. Julie
2. Pierre		2. Lise		2. Cathia	
3. Daniel		3. Karen		3. Anie	
4. Hélène				4. Éric	
5. Guy					

In 1897, Pit took his father's place as ambulance driver, carter, and boatman. He was always willing to help and his nature was as wholesome as the bread his brother Johnny made. He took the time to be nice to everyone. Here is an example. We lived in the last house of the lower row, so when Pit Masson, delivering the supplies ordered from Quebec or Montmagny, finally arrived at our door, what was left in the cart had to be for us. My little brothers would go out to see if we had any packages, and Pit Masson would pretend to check and give them one package. "It's for us," they would say, running into the house. They would go back out, and Pit Masson would continue playing the game until the cart was empty. He knew it made my brothers happy to discover our packages one at a time. A mere detail, you will tell me, but unexpected pleasures and moments of wonder are what brighten our lives.

Mr. and Mrs. Pierre (Pit) Masson were respected and admired by all those who knew them.

His son Freddy, third-generation Masson on Grosse Ile, was the island superintendent until May 1980. He was a very nice, affable, and dedicated man. Many others besides me can vouch for his good disposition and his kindness. Freddy did his father proud and was a true son of the island.

Although Joseph Masson did not live on the island, he is almost as much a part of its history as his two brothers. He was a doctor in Montmagny. Most importantly, he was the only doctor willing to cross the river through the ice floes in winter to assist women in labor and to treat sick people on Grosse Ile and Ile aux Grues.

Éméril told me that his uncle Joseph Masson, Member of Parliament for Montmagny and physician, burned an impressive stack of patients' unpaid bills when he moved to Montreal. Éméril was there when he did it. "That's one less problem for all of us," his uncle said. "Neither they nor I will have to worry about that money."

Our kindly Dr. Joseph Masson in his Saint Lazare office before he came to settle in Montmagny.

Jean-Baptiste (Johnny) Masson and Éléonore Delorme at the time of their wedding in 1897.

And I come to Johnny Masson. Let me tell you briefly how he met your grandmother, Éléonore Delorme of Aylmer. In 1883, she came to Grosse Ile for a visit with some friends, Dr. Church's family. They were adolescents. She was sixteen, and your grandfather, fourteen.

In 1897, she came back to the island with the same family, and on the boat, she met Johnny who was coming to visit his parents. Just as in any novel with a happy ending, they took to each other. A few months later, Father Derome, the pastor of Grosse Ile, married them in the island's little chapel. They lived happily ever after and had nine children, including your father Éméril.

Johnny had learned his trade at the Valiquette bakery. Afterward, he worked at Dupéré's. In 1905, he took over from his father as Grosse Ile's baker.

In addition to being a baker, Johnny was also well educated. I know that he went to a commercial school. I suppose he chose to come back to the island of his childhood, which was a nice place to live despite the isolation in winter.

I will say it again, all the Massons on the island were good people. They lived wholesomely. They were rather well-off, but did not consider money as a god. I think they understood life and lived in harmony with it.

Johnny and Éléonore Masson in front of the bakery in 1908.

Needless to say that after all those years on Grosse Ile, the Massons were well known there. In my day, Johnny was a little bit like the owner of the island, a father figure, and the host one might say. And your grandmother helped him a lot with his work. Facing the lower wharf, their house was the meeting place for important visitors. When government inspectors came on official business or to go fishing, it was almost always Johnny and his wife who provided the meals.

During the four months of isolation, Mrs. Johnny Masson became the islanders' sole nurse. During the summer, the doctors gave her much advice. If a woman was about to give birth, they sent for Mrs. Masson and told her what had to be done, in case she had to deliver a baby by herself — which happened a few times. Later in St. Clothilde, after I got married, she gave me the same advice, which proved very useful. Twice I found myself alone with a woman about to give birth. When the doctor arrived, the baby was already born.

Johnny was a boatman in winter, but foremost, he was Grosse Ile's baker. He was paid two hundred dollars for the boating season in winter and sixty dollars a month to bake. His bake oven adjoined his house. The government supplied the flour. Johnny had to bake a certain number of 5-pound loaves with each barrel of flour. Each family was charged for their bread. The bill was given to the superintendent, Dr. Martineau. The amount owed by each employee was deducted from his pay at the end of the month. The number of loaves baked for the hospital was also carefully recorded. Since we were charged for our bread, I never knew how much a loaf of bread cost on Grosse Ile! There was obviously always a little flour left. The government knew that and gave Johnny permission to bake and sell off the surplus for his own gain. Johnny then baked delicious little buns, doughnuts, and butter cookies which we fetched after church on Sundays and which Johnny *gave* us with a warm smile. That is the way those good people were.

For the feast of St. Catherine, on November 25, Johnny baked a huge batch of molasses taffy. That explains the peck of molasses he bought before the winter. Without being formally invited, almost all the youths gathered at Johnny Masson's house on the evening of the 25th. Ah, those big, beautiful twisted ropes of taffy that Johnny made! Every child went home with a piece of taffy, and Johnny always sent Papa a big, beautiful rope.

Starting in 1913, Johnny Masson's family lived in an addition to the bakery.

A baker in such an isolated place as Grosse Ile was a sort of symbol. Thanks to him, despite the isolation, the head of each family could bless the bread at every meal. Everyone on Grosse Ile made the same gesture of faith, a mystical link. The aroma of good, wholesome bread was reassuring; it was as much a part of our lives as the wind, the tide, the sun, the rain, and the seasons' passing.

I was at the bakery one day when Dr. Martineau walked in, his smile half embarrassed, half apologetic. He said to Johnny Masson, "New summer employees have told me that you cheat, that your loaves weigh less than they ought to. So I have to check."

He then took six loaves of bread from the shelves and weighed them. Each one was well over five pounds.

"I knew everything was in order," Dr. Martineau said then, "but it was my duty to check. I will put a stop to that malicious gossip!"

Those new summer employees certainly did not know the Massons well yet!

Talking about Johnny Masson, Mother used to say, "If the gift of a mere glass of water shall have its reward, think what reward Johnny Masson shall have for all those gallons of water he brought us." During our first two years on the island, there was no running water in winter — why? I cannot remember. During those first two winters, Papa suffered from rheumatism so badly that he could not walk. Mother was a tiny woman and not very strong since the birth of her last child. As for us children, we were too young to carry the water. So Johnny Masson did it and brought in the firewood as well! Mr. Jos Brautigam often gave him a hand with this good deed. It is impossible to forget such good people.

An addition was built to the bakery in 1913. Johnny Masson and his family lived there until 1922.

THE VEKEMAN FAMILY

My father — Gustaaf Vekeman — was born on September 12, 1841, in Zottegem, Belgium. He studied at the university of Louvain in Belgium. In Canada, his first name became Gustave.

He was a writer and a newspaperman. He loved to travel. He started a newspaper in every place he stayed for more than a year, so he is credited with a dozen newspapers. His taste for adventure brought him to Sherbrooke, Canada, in 1882. He then started writing to Belgium to give would-be Belgian immigrants information about the advantages of life in Canada. But this was not the only way he helped them; he also sent money.

Papa wrote for various Canadian newspapers, signing himself Jean des Érables. At the same time, another writer of newspaper articles in Quebec, Clara Rousseau, was signing herself Jeanne des Érables. An intriguing coincidence! Naturally they were curious to meet each other, and when they did, they fell in love. On April 19, 1897, they got married in Mother's native parish, Stanfold (now called Princeville). Afterward, they settled in Woonsocket, U.S.A., where Papa started a newspaper called *La Cloche du Dimanche (The Sunday Bell)*. I was born in that town on November 28, 1899. In 1902, we moved to Trois-Rivières, and finally, in 1907, to my dear Grosse Ile.

Gustave Vekeman's family during our stay on Grosse Ile. My mother, my father, and to my left, my brothers Gustave, Isidore, and Léon.

There were four Vekeman children. I was the oldest; Léon, only a year and a half my junior, soon joined other boys his age, sharing in their games. When he had turned thirteen, he pursued his studies as a boarder with the Fathers of the Sacred Heart. Since Isidore and Gustave were six and seven years my junior, I often played mother with them. I would watch them so they would not wander too far away from the house. Gustave was rather quiet and a little sickly. Early in his life he displayed a leaning towards reading. As for Isidore, what an adventurous spirit. I, for one, rescued him three times from certain death.

The first time, he was eighteen months old. We had gone on a picnic at the little ridge near Pit Masson's house. He slipped away and ended up falling into a stream. He had acted so fast, no one had noticed anything. When Mother realized that he was gone, we set out to look for him. I found him hanging on to the wooden transverse beams of the bridge spanning the stream. He was half drowned. Mother undressed him and wrapped him in Papa's coat.

Another time, the tide was beginning to ebb. Isidore was sitting astride a fallen tree trunk, clutching its few remaining branches with both hands. He was riding away like some horseman on his steed. I grabbed him just in time. I was not very tall, and the water was already becoming too deep for me. Imagine what would have happened if I had not been able to reach him. Before I could have alerted the men of the island, Isidore would have been carried away by the ebb current or would have fallen off his mount.

But who knows if I did not kill his taste for discovery right there and then. So many countries still unknown because of what I did!

One beautiful Sunday afternoon, my brothers and I went for a walk with some cousins of ours who had come to visit us on the island. We ended up at the foot of the well-known Irish memorial.

As was then in fashion, Isidore was wearing a sailor suit and a boater. A gust of wind blew his boater off and carried it along almost to the edge of the cliff. Isidore ran after it. Just as he was bending down to pick it up, the wind blew it over the edge, and Isidore dashed forward, yelling, "My hat! My hat!"

How I managed to hold him back and how we both found ourselves steady on our feet on solid ground I will never know. To think, if he had fallen over the edge, he would have dropped one hundred feet! A few days before, one of the men working on the monument had fallen off there and had been killed.

Dearest Isidore, will you be angry if I now mention your resourcefulness? Do you remember when you used our beautiful lace curtains to make a fishing net for minnows? You took care to hang them back in place — weeds, mud, pebbles, and all. You were treated to a *déjeuner causerie* (a good talking-to), and deservedly so!

Being the oldest entailed some obligations; I had to watch over my little brothers and set an example. One time, during lunch, Léon and I were picking on each other, just for fun. Then it became serious. I was really mean and offended Léon, who got angry and called me a name which Papa did not like in the least.

"Apologize to Jeannette immediately," he said to Léon, "You don't call your sister by a name like that."

Léon did as he was told, and Papa turned to me.

"It's your fault if your brother lost his temper; you provoked him. That's often how never-ending family quarrels get started. As a penance, you are to go up to your room *without dessert!*"

The real punishment was not being sent to my room, it was having to go without dessert. We never had any during the week, except fruit, molasses, or cookies. I could not imagine what regal dessert there had been at lunch that day! No one told me, and I did not ask any questions — that was the punishment! Just like losing the chance to win the grand prize which I will talk about further one.

Papa never struck us, but he had a way to make us do what he wanted without giving orders. He would say, "Son, you can bring in an armful of wood for your mother. It's too heavy for her." As for Mother, she would say, "My girl, your father will soon be here for supper, so would you set the table, please."

Only once did I see Mother angry — and then not very angry. She had been given a scare by her little ones, and felt she ought to teach them a lesson. They had managed to steal a few matches and had lit a fire under our back porch. Dry weeds and wood shavings were burning joyously. Fortunately, I was always on the watch. I quickly put out the fire, then told Mother about it. I was no tattletale, but this time, she had to speak to them. Can you imagine the consequences if I had not found them out; the whole row would have caught fire.

She made quite a production of it. She had me bring out a chair for her to sit in while she dispensed justice. She had the children stand on either side and told me to fetch a *little* stick. I was reluctant to obey.

"If I fetch it myself," said Mother, "it will be bigger!"

I then understood that I had to choose a small one — a very small one! *Holding the little stick in her little hands, Mother hit my little brothers a little bit on their little behinds.* They cried a lot, and I cried even more. It was such a solemn affair, this court of justice in the backyard at the end of the porch. Mother made my brothers see that their innocent fire could have had tragic consequences for all the tenants of the row and that the superintendent could have ordered us off the island.

Being the oldest also meant having certain privileges. I had a say in certain matters, and I was in on the secret when my parents were preparing surprises for the little ones' birthdays. Besides that, Papa would bring me along when he went to Quebec, and buy me some treats. We always went to the Garneau bookstore where he would buy me some books, drawing paper, and coloring pencils. It was a way to reward me for the things I did at home.

I was sturdy and quite strong for my age, so instinctively I always pushed myself forward. Without really knowing why, I wanted men and women to be equal. Whenever I brought in some wood in my wheelbarrow, I carried as much as the neighborhood boys, and I could hold my own against anyone of them my age. It was not beyond me to bring in wood, carry water for the vegetable patch, or dig in the garden. I did only what I could and wanted to do. It was good exercise. Girls today work much harder to win Olympic medals. I never got any medals, but my chores did me just as much good. And I still had ample time to play, skip rope, and daydream sitting on the rocks. I was proud of what I could do — perhaps a bit too proud.

When we were very young, we did our homework right after supper and then went to sleep early. We were tired. Besides having gone to school, we had played outside, either near the water's edge or in the snow, depending on the season. When we became older, Papa often told us stories. He was very learned. He shared his knowledge with us in a most pleasant way. Gathered around him in the heart of the house, we hung on his every word.

He had written a book — *Les Histoires de Grand-Père Caron (Grandfather Caron's Stories)* — a collection of his first wife's father's war stories. I was never able, however, to find this book. Papa also told us about the Chouan insurrection and the Boer war. He told us that some French noblemen had immigrated to America to flee from the revolution. Many a nobleman was saved by a loyal servant. My little brothers would fall asleep, but I was older and often worried during those stories. I wanted to know if this or that character in Papa's story would manage to escape safely.

"Is there a good villain?" I would ask Papa.

"Yes, of course," he would say. "Rest easy, Jeannette; there is a good villain."

It was the loyal servant!

Papa received many almanacs as well as French and Belgian magazines containing such things as the legends of Saints and the traditions of holy days.

For example, we read that in Brittany, on the eve of All Souls' Day, people built small boats, put candles on them, and set them afloat. The boats drifted with the current, while the people on the shore recited some prayers for the souls of the mariners lost at sea.

And there was the legend of St. Nicholas. The good saint stopped by with his donkey during the night from the fifth to the sixth of December. Expecting his visit, children had taken care to put a carrot in a box at the foot of their beds for St. Nicholas' donkey. A surprise always awaited them come morning; the carrot had disappeared, replaced by some sweets and fruit. When we were little, this custom was observed. You were also just as happy, on the morning of December 6, to find some peanuts and homemade maple cream fudge in your boxes — remember?

There was also the beautiful Easter legend. On Maundy Thursday, the bells left for Rome to be blessed and returned on Easter Sunday. On the way back, they dropped Easter eggs in people's gardens. In Europe, parents hid the eggs in the flowerbeds. In Canada, that was a problem because of the snow! In our family, we found the Easter eggs on the lunch table in beautiful china eggcups.

When Papa was not telling stories, Mother was reading to us in her beautiful voice from texts which were well written and full of useful information. As soon as she began to read, we were spellbound. Her expressive voice made the stories come to life.

In winter, Papa organized a lottery at the end of every month, if we had been good. We had to bring in the wood, shovel the porch, pump the water, help Mother. The prizes were four identical handfuls of candies. Our names were written on four pieces of paper and placed in Papa's cap. The one whose name was drawn first won the grand prize, *the privilege of being the first* to receive his handful of candies!

And from one month to the next, we dreamt of being the lucky grand prize winner. How simple happiness is! Were we naive? In our early years, I suppose we were. But how beautiful it is to remember that ritual which was used by Papa to teach us that happiness is something one can easily create.

On one occasion, my brother Gustave had talked about it to a neighbor, Lucien Hamel. On the afternoon of the draw, Lucien turned up at our house. He envied us for having so many treats and was hoping to take part in the lottery. He stared wide-eyed at the four rows of candies.

"Shall we make a row for Lucien?" I said to Papa.

"Certainly," he said.

I fetched another handful of candies, and whose name should come out first but Lucien's!

"Lucien has won the grand prize!" we cried all at once.

Lucien took everything on the table, the five rows of candies. He certainly had caught on fast!

On our birthday, we got a little cake. On the feast day of our patron saint, there was a bigger celebration, and Papa told us the story of our patron saint. The feast day of my brother Isidore's patron saint was on April 4 — it has been moved since then. One year, he had just received his usual treat, and Gustave, who was younger, thought Isidore was very lucky. "When is my April 4?" he asked Papa. It has remained a family joke. Whenever someone's birthday is being celebrated, our wishes go like this: "On the occasion of your April 4" and so forth. How we loved our patron saints! We would have liked to have all the saints as our patrons!

In winter, Papa had some spare time. He had taken woodworking courses in Belgium. In the summer, the hospital's supplies came in huge wooden crates. Once they were empty, people used them to fuel their stoves. Papa used to pick out the best pieces to build things with.

He made replicas of the Grotto at Lourdes for the island's yearlong residents. These grottos were three feet high. The statue of the Virgin stood fifteen inches high, and that of St. Bernadette kneeling was in proportion. Papa also made a bigger grotto for the school. I gave him a lot of help making the grottos; I was his assistant woodworker! It was I who plastered and painted. I set pebbles in the plaster to make it look more real. Indeed I quite enjoyed building things with Papa. That is why I knew how to drill holes with an auger to let the water run out after the famous "great tide" and why I knew how to plug the holes with an old broomstick!

I do not know what became of the school's grotto. Papa had also built a small portable throne on which sat a statue of Our Lady of the Sacred Heart. Mother had covered the throne with some ruffled light blue tulle sprinkled with gold sequins and had put a garland of flowers at the foot of the statue. Four little girls in white dresses and long veils bore the throne during the Corpus Christi procession, while four others held blue ribbons.

Where are those things today? Oh how I would love to find those mementos of my childhood, now twice as dear to this grandmother's heart!

Papa had built a nice little chest of drawers for my dolls' clothes, some cupboards for Mother, and several little tables. He had set up a workbench in one of the upstairs bedrooms. The boys, and especially Isidore, wanted to build things and used Papa's plane in a most unorthodox way. Even after numerous lessons on its proper handling, Isidore still planed the heads of nails with it. Finally Papa said, "Don't touch my plane anymore. If you are a good boy, you will get your very own plane someday." And then weeks went by. Sometimes, when Isidore misbehaved, Papa would say to him, "Your plane is drawing away."

So it turned out that the plane "drew away" more often than not, and Papa died before he could give Isidore a plane. One of my daughters, who knew the story, found a beautiful plane in an antique shop and gave it to Isidore for his 73rd birthday. He was thrilled; he had longed for and dreamt about that plane for such a long time.

In the summer, the public works employees found Sundays away from their families long and boring. Their foreman asked Papa to come speak before them. So Papa lectured to them several times, on various topics such as: the war, Joan of Arc, and Napoleon. He was an accomplished speaker, interesting to listen to and so knowledgeable that people drank in his every word. I tagged along with Papa, dear Papa.

In 1914, Papa started his last newspaper. It was in fact a monthly periodical despite its name: *Le Journal des Enfants (The Children's Journal)*. Written and illustrated by and for the children, this monthly bore some resemblance to *Crayons de Soleil*, the supplement of the newspaper *Le Soleil*. Children from several colleges, convents, academies, and other schools from all over Quebec and even from Manitoba and the United States contributed eagerly.

Laflamme's printers, then located at 34 Garneau Street in Quebec, printed the paper and served as a "mailbox" for the letters addressed to it.

Since *Le Journal des Enfants* had only two editors, my parents, they used various pen names. Papa signed himself Jean Canada, Père Marie-Antoine (in my honor!), Michel, or Amicus; while Mother signed herself Spes, and La Direction (The Editors). Father Paré also wrote short articles signed M.P. Aunt Eugénie chose the winners of the various contests.

The paper was published for two years. Papa, then seventy-five years old and ailing, had to give it up to the great disappointment of his subscribers. A complete, twelve-issue collection of *Le Journal des Enfants* is kept at the National Library in Montreal.

Papa was an accomplished speaker, interesting to listen to and so knowledgeable that people drank in his every word. And I tagged along with him.

Papa also wrote occasionally for several European newspapers, and once a week, for *Le Courrier de Montmagny*. I found a complete collection of *Le Courrier de Montmagny* from 1906 to 1908 at the National Library in Quebec. Papa signed his articles either G.V., Gustave Vekeman, Jean des Érables, or L'ami de l'ouvrier (The workman's friend).

One winter, he sent a seventy-part serial novel entitled *Les Vipères* (*The Vipers*) to *De Zondagbode* (*Sunday Mail*), a newspaper in Zottegem, Belgium. At the end of the last episode, Papa had signed "Gustaaf Vekeman, Grosse Ile, October 20, 1908."

Papa also did some translation for the *Canada Gazette*. Translators in those days were paid a dollar a page, and Papa sometimes made up to fifty dollars a year. Because he was not paid in wintertime, this extra income was important to our family. Sometimes, Papa made us pray for Ottawa to send him some translations to do.

Usually it was I who fetched the mail, and when I saw a government envelope, I would run home shouting, "Papa, Papa, translations!" I knew he would give us some small treats once he had received his check. Papa spoke and wrote French well except that he addressed everyone as "vous" including his wife and children. We, of course, were used to it and did not notice it, but it always surprised strangers a little bit.

If we were rowdy while Papa was writing his newspaper articles, he would say, "Children, be quiet and odorless!" Ow! We looked at each other sideways. "Quiet," we understood; but "odorless?" What could it possibly mean? So we stood still for fear of not being odorless! But we would soon resume our boisterous games. "If I get angry," Papa would say then, "I'll make it hot for you!" Just to be on the safe side, we took off one sweater so we would not get too warm! The third warning was, "Children, don't make me blow my top!" That was as far as it went. We did not know what it meant, but we would never have dared make him blow his top. The very idea scared us stiff! We were very young; to see Papa blow his top, not on your life! Unconsciously or not, we always played the game until Papa gave us the third and terrifying warning!

Though he would tolerate rowdiness, he never allowed fighting. We could be rambunctious, but Papa said fighting always led to unnecessary grief. To tell the truth, we were rather quiet. Mother and Papa were both rather calm people. As youngsters, we were playful, but later on, we often talked with them about literature, science, history, and other topics.

My parents had bought me a harmonium and arranged for Father Paré to give me music lessons. In 1914, I started to accompany the hymn singing in the chapel during services, benedictions of the Blessed Sacrament, and evening prayers. I practiced a lot at home. My mother and my brothers would often gather around, and my practicing would turn into a family sing-along.

My mother, Clara Rousseau Vekeman

In memory of those pleasant evenings and in gratitude to Mother for all the things she did in those years after Papa's death, here is a favorite song of hers, which describes her so well.

"Talking of my Mother"

<table>
<tr><td>1</td><td>2</td></tr>
</table>

1

When young I had my mother
Oh! Always shall I remember
Ne'er did the slightest sorrow
Cast a shadow over me
In our small village, my mother
Had nothing except her work
And there were four of us children
Who were never left wanting.

2

Mother said that only work
To better days could lead the way
The lazy get only hay
To the reapers grain befalls
Poor was she but rich with kindness
Often she told her children,
"People grow richer when giving"
Oh, how rich our mother grew!

Chorus: Her memory do I treasure
             Though I am now so far along in years
             See dear children when I talk of her   ⎫
             My eyes become filled with tears.   ⎬ bis
                                                ⎭

3

In her humble little house
She read us the Bible's treasures
Then she had us recite our prayers
In those days, how well we prayed
I hear her telling me often,
"In this world be not greedy
Always work hard and be honest
That is what God teaches us."

I am telling you all this so you will realize that our life on Grosse Ile was much like that of all chidren the world over. It was a life full of joys, sorrows, hopes, and dreams. The training our parents gave us and the beauty of the island combined to give us a deep appreciation of life.

Later on, when I ran into the concrete wall erected by human stupidity, my heart, bound by memories of Grosse Ile, could not swell with hatred. And for that, I thank my upbringing.

Papa, who spoke eight languages well and could make himself understood in at least half a dozen others, spent his days at the hospital. He accompanied the nurses as they tended the sick and explained the treatments and medications to the patients. He always had to be available, in case a communication problem arose.

Papa died in 1916 at the age of seventy-five. He had been showing signs of weakness and fatigue for some time. He also had digestive problems, and working all day was sometimes hard on him. For the last two years of his life, it was Mother who wrote his articles for *Le Courrier de Montmagny*. Papa would outline the topic he wanted to discuss and Mother would write the article.

Probably sensing that the end was near, Papa said to me one day, "Jeannette, I'm counting on you to help your mother raise your little brothers." I looked at Papa in surprise, but something told me that he was very serious and that a formal reply would reassure him. So I said, "Yes, Papa. I shall do my best."

And in all honesty, I believe I have kept my promise as well as I could.

There came a time when Papa experienced dizzy spells and temporary partial paralyses. After one of those attacks of paralysis, Dr. Martineau said to Mother, "Mrs. Vekeman, you are not a child so I feel it is my duty to tell you that your husband has only a couple of weeks left to live."

How hard it was for Mother to see the end draw near, unable to make time stand still and determined to keep the truth from her children.

Papa worked at the hospital up to the end. On the morning of Wednesday the fifth of July, 1916, he did not wake up. He had died peacefully and given up his soul to eternity.

Dear Papa! The story of your stay on the island is an important chapter in its history for all concerned, islanders as well as immigrants.

Time will never erase the memory of my islands.

ILE SAINTE-MARGUERITE

MY GOING FROM CHILDHOOD TO ADULTHOOD

After Papa's death, Odilon Pruneau asked Mother if she would allow me to go teach his children. The Pruneau family, living alone on Ile Sainte-Marguerite, included several children of school age. That year, they had been granted an allowance by the government to help pay a teacher.

It was an unexpected opportunity for me. I was happy since I was not leaving my islands and I was going to stay with people I knew well. It made being away from my family more bearable — and living in the city did not appeal to me. Aside from my sorrow over the loss of my father and the separation from my family, it was a truly wonderful year for me.

The Pruneaus lived in a gambrel-roofed house, warm, roomy, sturdy, and well-lit by about ten high windows. Downstairs there were a huge kitchen, the grandparents' bedroom, and the dining room. Upstairs were four large bedrooms. The attic served as a pantry in winter. Almost all of the furniture was handmade — nothing fancy, I admit, but everything always spick-and-span.

A hand pump supplied the water. There were a summer kitchen and a bread oven adjoining the house. The telephone, recently installed on Ile Sainte-Marguerite, gave one a feeling of security.

On Ile Sainte Marguerite, the Pruneaus lived in a large, sturdy, gambrel-roofed house.

The Pruneaus were good people, well brought up, sociable, and tactful. Mrs. Odilon Pruneau, Johnny Masson's sister, was well educated. Before her marriage, she had been a telegrapher on Grosse Ile. I immediately felt at ease with her and the entire household. They were all very good to me and did their best, I now realize, to ease my homesickness. I quickly adapted to their way of life which, on the whole, was not all that different from the one on Grosse Ile. In fact, the only difference was that because this family lived alone on their island, they sometimes had to make do with what was available.

The boys' bedroom served as a classroom during the day. I was following the current school program. Classes were held from 9:00 to 11:30 a.m. and from 1:00 to 3:30 p.m. In the morning, after a prayer, we had a catechism lesson. I remembered very well what the pastor had taught me in catechism to prepare for my solemn communion. Then we moved on to the other subjects. My pupils were quiet, studious, polite, and well behaved.

What did they call me? "Miss" was a little too formal, it would have made people ill at ease; "Jeannette" was too familiar where my pupils were concerned. Then Mrs. Pruneau settled the matter — I would be called "Teacher." This allowed our relations to be cordial without compromising my authority.

In winter it gets dark early and the sandman soon comes. After supper, once the dishes were done, the children gathered around the big table for a game of cards or something else; then they cleaned themselves up, said a prayer, and went to bed.

The adults stayed up a while longer, talking about one thing or another: the weather, the condition of the river, the latest news from the papers (we were then right in the middle of the War of 1914-18), conscription, the Russian revolution. The men smoked their pipes; the women took advantage of the rest of the evening to knit, mend clothes, and peel potatoes for the next day. Later we went to sleep with an easy conscience. Were there not sixteen guardian angels watching over this isolated family, away from everything and living alone in the only house on Ile Sainte-Marguerite, an island lost in midstream?

We rose early on the island. First thing in the morning, Odilon did the chores with his old father. Then we had breakfast and a little later classes began for the children. As in any busy hive, everyone had a job to do.

Life was simple and patriarchal — or rather matriarchal since it was the grandmother who reigned supreme over the house and family. She was the "strong woman" referred to in the Bible, and I mean that as a compliment. Let us say that there were two strong women, Ruth and Naomi, walking hand in hand. But one hive cannot have two queens, and in the hive of Ile Sainte-Marguerite, the older woman wore the crown. The young one, however, was also fit to rule, but for the sake of harmony she yielded to her elder. As a result, everything was well organized, without stringency or monotony. The children, being congenial by nature, played together happily; and being well behaved, they put away their toys when they finished. The Pruneaus' was a happy household.

Odilon, a progressive man, took the advice of the agronomist from Montmagny on how to run his farm. He was a member of the *Cercle du contrôle laitier* which regularly ran tests to control the quality of the milk. He earned part of his income selling wholesome butter at seventeen cents a pound. Enough to become rich!

He often crossed over to Ile aux Grues or to Grosse Ile to hear Mass and, while there, to trade his produce for supplies and to pick up the mail.

There was always some repair work to be done around the buildings, and the house and the boats often needed refitting. Odilon made and mended the sails of his boats himself. He was a welder, a plumber, and a tinsmith, all trades he had worked at in Quebec before his father turned over to him the management of the island's farm.

The elder man, however, still had a say in things. He was a sweet old indulgent grandfather who knew what he wanted, but was neither dead set in his opinions nor domineering. He was attentive to his wife and helped his daughter-in-law with a lot of chores too tiring for a woman who had a baby every year. He was still active. He and his aging brother Joseph saw to the heating of the house. They kept a good supply of wood for the kitchen stove and the bread oven by gathering driftwood. From year to year, there was always a big stack of it left out to dry, neatly piled near the house.

It also fell to the grandfather to look after the moccasin-like "Indian boots" and the leather mittens. Using a paintbrush, he impregnated them with hot seal oil to keep them supple and waterproof for the canoe trips. The boots and mittens were made by the women of the household. They taught me how to sew them. They also made overalls and oilskins from un-bleached, close-textured cotton, previously shrunk. Each item was lined with the same fabric and sewn in such a way as to be reversible.

Once that was done, the grandfather stepped in. He soaked each piece in a big kettle filled with hot oil, stirring them to make sure they were thoroughly permeated with oil. He then wrung them out and hung them on the clothesline to dry. Afterwards, he stirred some water, nails, and vitriol in a tin vessel, which gave a nice black dye. Still using a brush, he painted each piece with dye, let them dry once more, and that was it! Everyone had supple, durable, waterproof clothes.

I took part in all those operations, and I learned a lot. It was wonder-ful to see just how well those people managed and how self-sufficient they were, isolated from everyone and everything. They believed in doing things well.

On Ile Sainte-Marguerite, I saw some beautiful and sturdy carts and wheels made by the Pruneaus. There were also finely crafted wooden yokes, leather harnesses for the draft oxen, wool spools, butter prints and presses, wooden spoons and plates, dark-colored chairs with geometrical patterns made up of leather thongs, hand tools, and linen chests.

I was fascinated by the large bread bin, the cradle — in which many a little Pruneau was rocked to sleep — and the windmill for threshing, with sails like dragonflies dancing in the wind.

In the spring, the sheep were sheared. Carefully selected, the wool had to be washed and carded. Long staple wool, from the back and sides, would be used to knit socks, mittens, and sweaters because it felted less. Short staple wool, from the neck, abdomen, and upper legs, was blended with long wool and used to weave blankets and sheets. Long wool, turned into fine-spun yarn, also served for flannel for underclothes. They may have been a little scratchy, but they were warm in winter and helped keep the blood moving!

Whenever possible, one or two white fleeces were blended with a black one to get a nice gray color which did not show the dirt and did not need to be dyed. The Pruneaus had once grown some flax and rye on the island, but had later given it up.

In winter, the women spun, wove, and sewed. They made quilts and braided carpets. As for the men, they repaired their tools and prepared them for the coming summer. Mrs. Odilon Pruneau had the skin of a sheep or calf tanned and made rather pretty little shoes for the children six and under, and occasionally, for the older ones too. The Pruneaus had everything a shoemaker might need: lasts of all sizes, awls, wax thread, pitch, wax, and coal tar mixed together to waterproof the wax thread. Once in a while, Mrs. Pruneau even made "Sunday" shoes with heels. You could have sworn they were store-bought!

As you can see, there was no unemployment on the island, nor were there any strikes. People did not have time to think about such things.

In the fall, the men slaughtered pigs, lambs, poultry, and cattle and sold some of the meat on Grosse Ile. They put the surplus pork fat in salt. This preserved it for eating during the summer, for there were no icehouses on Ile Sainte-Marguerite in those days.

The two Pruneau women were expert cooks. The grandmother baked pastries, pies, cakes, meat pies, cookies, and other desserts. The younger woman cooked the meat and prepared soups, vegetables, stews, and Canada goose pies. She also baked three batches of bread every other week — eight to ten big loaves. She made her own yeast with real hops and boiled potatoes. This gave a light, fine-textured, and delicately flavored bread which we ate with delicious butter. Mrs. Pruneau had learned how to bake bread from her brother, Johnny Masson, when she was still living on Grosse Ile. She used the same oven to prepare delicious baked beans. I should also mention the raspberry syrup they made and reserved for holidays and special occasions. There was always plenty of delicious food on the Pruneaus' table — nothing precooked, everything homemade. And I was forgetting the soap. Oh yes, the Pruneau women also made their own soap!

The main source of income on the island was the potato crop. The fall crop of 1916 was a record one: a hundred sacks more than the most optimistic predictions. At one dollar a sack, it rather helped to pay the teacher's salary! I received one hundred dollars for the year; fifty dollars from the government and fifty dollars from Odilon Pruneau.

It took at least two weeks to dig the potatoes. The children made up a good portion of the manpower, so school was out for the duration. The teacher was inevitably on vacation. But I just could not stay idle. And since I liked the outdoors, I helped harvest the potatoes; it was an experience for me. We really had a good time doing it; everyone was in good and high spirits. We did not mind the hours. We had to take advantage of the fine weather to do the harvesting which, in fact, became a picnic, a real rural festival.

Then around mid-November, if I remember correctly, the Pruneaus welcomed their ninth child into the world. The baby, a handsome, big, healthy boy, had a strong will to live so its baptism was postponed until later.

Time was short, Odilon had to bring his potato crop upriver as soon as possible before the river froze over. Besides, the first ones to arrive in Quebec were always sure to sell their stock of potatoes, butter, eggs, and other farm produce at the highest prices. Boats, schooners, and yachts berthed at the Louise Basin. Merchants hopped aboard to inspect the cargo. If it was to their liking, they bought and always for a higher price than at the end of the trading season. That particular fall, Odilon Pruneau had a very good trip.

He came back to Ile Sainte-Marguerite, his yacht loaded with enough bulk supplies to last for at least six or seven months. Everything had been bought by the hundred pounds or by the crateful. Besides the bulk goods, he brought some personal things. There were a few yards of cotton fabric for the women of the house to make some aprons and dresses. I received a blouse length. The boys got two-blade pocketknives and store-bought sweaters, and the girl, Bernadette, a pretty little handbag. Mr. Pruneau also brought back some mysterious packages for the Holidays, one of which contained a five-dollar bill for me!

December. It was now time to go to Grosse Ile to have the last baby baptized. There was already some ice drifting on the river. The two Pruneau men, Arthur Masson (Éméril's brother), and I, holding the warmly bundled baby, crossed over to Grosse Ile. I was sitting in the bottom of the boat on a big blanket made up of four sheepskins. I pulled the sides of it over the baby, and wrapped warmly in this golden fleece, we were ready to face the bitterest cold. That day, however, the weather was fine. We left with the rising tide. After the baptism, we ate a light lunch at Johnny Masson's and then we hurried back to Ile Sainte-Marguerite to take advantage of the ebbing tide. The Pruneau family now boasted one more little Christian named Philippe.

The days went by peacefully, uneventfully, and Christmas was soon upon us. The elder Pruneaus went to spend the Holidays on Ile aux Grues where four of their daughters lived. For his part, Édouard Masson came to spend Christmas with his daughter, the young Mrs. Pruneau. On December 24, Mr. Pruneau and his hired man crossed over to Grosse Ile with the rising tide to hear midnight Mass.

Old Uncle Joseph and the children went to sleep early. Mrs. Pruneau, her father, and I all stayed up, keeping the stove burning and chatting in low voices. I was thinking about my family, but without sadness. In spirit, we were together with the priest celebrating Mass on the neighboring island. Carols rang in our heads. The night was quiet and a multitude of stars lit up the sky — silent night, holy night — Christmas night!

"We too will have a midnight supper," Mrs. Pruneau said when the clock struck twelve. Then, sitting around a small table near the fire, we feasted on a midnight supper as extravagant as a millionaire might have had. There was plenty of broth, fresh bread with lots of butter on it, and doughnuts. Was that all, you ask? No. The most important thing was not what we ate, it was the love and warmth we felt; the happiness of a father and daughter reunited; and for me, something of my father and mother that I saw in them.

We stayed up like that until the break of day. After all, someone had to help the guardian angels watch over the sleeping children until the men returned.

The large Pruneau family was a picture of happiness.

Spring brought the end of Lent. The pastor of Ile aux Grues came to our island so we could make our Easter duty. If memory serves me right, it was Xavier Lachance and his friend, a Vézina, who manned the canoe on that trip. They arrived one fair afternoon. Until suppertime, Father Paré — the brother of the pastor of Grosse Ile — talked with the people of the house, inquiring about their health and taking an interest in the children. That priest knew how to make people feel at ease.

After supper, confessions were heard in the grandparents' room where there were a prie-dieu for the penitents and a chair for the priest. Afterwards, the priest gave Adrien, who was to make his first communion, the catechism examination.

The next day at seven o'clock, Father Paré said a Low Mass. The Pruneaus owned everything that was needed for a table altar: a knockdown table, a white altar cloth, a crucifix, candlesticks, altar cards, and so on. We all received communion, including young Adrien. After the office, the thanksgiving, and the homily, we ate a brunch. It was a wonderful meal, worthy of the finest tables and served with heartwarming cordiality.

A little more advice, a final blessing, a warm handshake from the priest, and the boatmen signalled that it was time to go. Since the river served as the islanders' road, people had to take advantage of favorable conditions to travel on it. Thus to return to Ile aux Grues, the boatmen had to take advantage of the ebbing tide.

Back at the house, we commented on that happy event which had left us with an indescribable feeling of inner peace. Our sins had been forgiven, and God was living in our hearts. "Lord, I am not worthy to have you come under my roof" — but He had come under the roof of those good people, the Pruneaus.

Then summer returned. Flowers once more dotted the newly green fields. May, June, and the school year ended. I left the Pruneaus and Ile Sainte-Marguerite to go live in Quebec with my family, reunited once more. Such happiness! But I nevertheless felt a pang when I left those fine people who had provided me with the warmth of a home during that year of transition.

All my life, I have had the fondest memories of them.

Ile Sainte-Marguerite served as a wonderful stepping-stone for me, allowing me to cross from childhood to adulthood. I was ready to take on my share of responsibilities and to live for the collective good, without signing a collective agreement!

Daisies, little flowers with white petals and golden hearts, which I sometimes pick, you always remind me of a certain year, perhaps the most enriching of my life.

LOVE

PRELUDE

In 1906, Papa had been hired to be an interpreter at the quarantine station. Not knowing what living conditions to expect there, he had gone ahead alone. Mother was pregnant so we stayed in our house in Trois-Rivières. With the help of an old neighbor, Mother cultivated vegetables in our huge garden and gathered delicious plums from the orchard. Taking her time, with the help of the neighbor's wife, she packed our belongings for the coming move to Grosse Ile. As for Papa, he boarded at Johnny Masson's for the season, and that was the beginning of a lasting friendship between the two families.

Papa decided, however, that it would be wiser for Mother not to come to the island that year. We went to Montmagny for the winter, and on October 17, my brother Gustave was born. Papa was still on Grosse Ile. Dr. Joseph Masson delivered the "gift from the Indians." I think he had signed a contract with them!

We spent the winter all together in Montmagny. Papa went to Grosse Ile during the Holiday Season to see how the people lived during those four months of isolation and cold. That was the trip he described in that article published in *Le Courrier de Montmagny*.

We lived on St. Jean Baptiste Street opposite the Laberge hardware store. The house still exists today. It has been moved a few feet to make room for a larger building. Dr. Masson and Dr. Richard lived nearby.

Together with Léon, I often fetched bread from the Fournier bakery. Occasionally, we stayed awhile to look after the children, Florence and Pierre, while Mrs. Fournier helped her husband put the loaves in the oven. Afterwards, Mrs. Fournier played the piano and her husband sang. We were delighted to hear them, especially since we also received a handful of candies as payment for having watched the children.

I also delivered Papa's articles to *Le Courrier de Montmagny* and fetched sewing articles from a Mrs. Soucy who also sold sweets. When we had been good, Papa would give Léon and me a nickel, and I would buy two little chocolate mice. Still, Papa did not spend a fortune on mice that winter! I also remember a Mrs. Bernatchez from whom we bought milk, and Roméo Lespérance, the grocer. I would give him the grocery list Mother had written down in a notebook, and a clerk would deliver everything to the house.

I bought butter at Tondreau's where Grosse Ile's people got their butter in winter. Mr. Tondreau was a member of the Montmagny brass band, and for years, that band came to give concerts on Grosse Ile in the summer. I also remember the Nicole's butcher shop, the Nicole's shoemaker shop, and the Michon's drugstore.

Once in a while, I went to the presbytery with Léon, and Father Marois, the pastor, would chat with us. One day, he had us come into his office to give us each an embossed color picture with a paper frame which looked like lace. He showed us a crucifix with a figure of Jesus the size of a child, and little goldfish in a big aquarium. Such amazing things for us!

Papa and Mother were our teachers during that winter, but my clearest memories are those of Mr. Johnny Masson's visits when he came to Montmagny to fetch the mail. He always impressed me with his gentle blue eyes, his brown hair and beard. He was almost as tall as Papa, but much more slender. He wore high, laced boots which came up to his thighs and which he called his boatman's boots.

A strong bond of friendship existed between Papa and Johnny Masson. Knowing that, I was already dreaming about Grosse Ile.

At the beginning of April 1907, Papa went back to work and we joined him at the end of the month. I remember the trip as if it were yesterday. To reach Grosse Ile, we first took the train to Lévis. From there, we traveled by boat to Quebec, where Papa was waiting for us. Then we boarded the *Contest*. The long journey on the water was wonderful.

Around 6 p.m., we finally reached Grosse Ile. We were starved and tired. Before Papa had left to meet us, Mrs. Johnny Masson had said to him, "Your wife and children will have supper here, and don't you argue." And so it was. We caught a glimpse of Johnny's children, but I was too tired to notice any one. Still, a vague image lingered in my mind.

LOVE AT FIRST SIGHT

IN A POOL OF WATER!

About two weeks after our arrival on the island, Mother paid a courtesy and thank you call to Mrs. Johnny Masson. While the two mothers were chatting, Léon and I were looking out the window at the little Massons and their friends who were playing in two large, shallow pools of water. They were floating little boats on the water and had installed miniature wharfs and seines made from burlap sacks. They seemed to be catching miraculous drafts of minnows.

"Take off your shoes," Mrs. Masson said to us, "and go play in the water with the others." She put Mother's mind at ease, telling her that there was no danger, that the tide was low. So we rushed outside, hand in hand. Playing barefoot was something new for us. Like runaway colts, we crashed our way through to the middle of the pools, breaking the wharfs, sinking the little boats, scaring away the minnows — those poor children had never seen such a tidal wave before. You can well image that they did not exactly welcome us with open arms. When the oldest made threatening gestures, our enthusiasm faded and we started to cry.

Then Éméril (seven and a half like me), the only one not yelling at us, took Léon and me by the hand. "Leave them alone," he said to the others, "they don't know yet about playing in puddles." He then said to us, "Come to the house; you'll come back another day and I'll play with you." At the house, he explained to both mothers why we were crying and why the others had given us a poor welcome.

Well! That is how I *fell in love at first sight*. But you know, once this happens, it changes you for life — and from that moment on, I thought that boy was ever so nice. I did not even know his name, but I could recognize him amongst the others.

AFTER LOVE AT FIRST SIGHT

A SWORD OF SORROW

September came. Léon and I started on the way to school for the first time. That too was new.

On the way, we would walk by the Brautigams' house and two boys would fall into step with us. Then further on, it would be the little Massons' turn. One morning, all of us stopped to chat awhile. It was getting late. From her doorstep, Mrs. Johnny Masson said to us, "Run along, children, it's late."

As we were taking our sweet time, she said louder, "Hurry up or I'll take you there myself. The teacher will punish you."

Then, the oldest of Johnny's children said, "The devil take the teacher."

And we all repeated, "The devil take the teacher!"

Who talked about that incident at school? Nobody knows. Nonetheless someone did tell the teacher, Miss X, about it, adding that Éméril had been the first one to say the disrespectful sentence. Investigation, inquisition. Éméril kept repeating that he had not started it, but without betraying the guilty party. I tried to deny it myself, to help the poor, innocent Éméril, but alas, I did not speak very loud and the others were crying, "Yes, Miss, it's him."

Everyone was glad to find a scapegoat and avoid punishment.

Then things got really bad. The teacher sent for Father Derome — the presbytery was only about a hundred feet from the school. She explained to him the case before the court and the pastor made a three-point sermon. Poor Éméril was forced to ask for forgiveness on his knees and to promise to show more respect for authority in the future, all the while crying his heart out. I too cried that day to see that innocent boy humiliated. Besides being so nice and helpful, he was now a martyr in my eyes — but I kept that to myself, deep in my heart. Little did I know on that day that I had just had a vision of what life would be like with Éméril, forever the good Samaritan taking upon himself other people's sorrows and misdeeds and paying the price for doing so. Dearest Éméril, how kind you have always been. But our children are your reward. They love you for your kindness, and I know that they thank you from the bottom of their hearts.

THE SWEET PLEASURE OF LOVE

Time passed without us giving it any thought. Éméril was top of the class amongst the boys, and I was at the head amongst the girls, except in mathematics.

Our last year in grade school together, on awards day in June 1913, there were two special awards — two five-dollar gold coins — one given by the inspector and the other by grandfather Édouard Masson. Those prizes for excellence went to the most deserving boy and girl of the class. The teacher, Aunt Eugénie, who had replaced Miss Grégoire in September 1911, held a secret vote. The boys voted for the girls, and the girls, for the boys. She had the students count the votes. Éméril won hands down on the boys' side, and I, on the girls' side.

The highlight of the celebration, after the performances, the recitations, and the songs, was the presentation of the special prizes. Éméril and I stood all alone in front on the platform, facing the audience, red as beets and uncomfortable in our little Sunday boots. We were proclaimed the heroes of the school year, and we each received a five-dollar gold coin. I was all the more thrilled because I was sharing the honor and the congratulations with the object of my love, Éméril.

It was the only time, from the day I fell in love at first sight in a pool of water to the day of our wedding, that we appeared together in public!

Then came summer vacation, carefree and bright as usual. Besides helping Mother at home and learning how to cook, sew, and embroider, I spent long hours by the water's edge, reading a book or observing nature. We sometimes talked together, the river and I. With difficulty did I drag myself away from the breathtaking scene of my little blue islands wrapped in sunlight and ethereal mist. I was happy.

Came September and a new school year. Éméril left for Ottawa to study at the Fathers of Mary Immaculate Conception boarding school and then at the University of Ottawa. He graduated with the degree of Bachelor of Arts. Sometimes he came back for the Holidays, sometimes he stayed with relatives in Ottawa. When he came back for summer vacation, he spent his time either on the water fishing or on Ile Sainte-Marguerite making hay with his uncle. He also helped a lot at home. He brought in the wood for the bakery oven, gave his mother a hand when she was cooking for the island's visitors, and looked after his young sisters and his baby brother Joseph.

We saw each other on the steps of the chapel on Sundays or at the bakery when he happened to be there handing out the bread. From one year to the next, obviously, we grew older; we were no longer children. We no longer played "tag," nor "four corners," nor "ferry." "Ferry?" Two lines of players faced each other, one player stood alone between the two lines. On each side, people signalled him discreetly to join them. The player ran to where he thought he would get a warm welcome. He was often mistaken; then he was out of the game and received a penalty.

The new school year always came too soon. I missed Éméril a lot, and time seemed to drag on without him on the island. Still, we saw little of each other when he was there and we spoke even less. I do not know what he thought, but silence often speaks louder than words.

When he left for the first time, in September 1913, several of his grade school friends and the teacher, my aunt, saw him off at the wharf, waving good-by to him when the *Alice* set off for Quebec. But I did not go. Walking past the bakery, I saw him standing on the threshold, ready to go — was he waiting for me? Not a word was said. We only nodded to each other and a long look passed between us which only God must have understood and of which He probably approved. I did not recognize it then, for I was only thirteen and a half, but my heart had told me, "Yes, for better or for worse — and forever." He headed for the wharf, and I hurried to the chapel for the seven o'clock Low Mass. The boat always left at seven, and when it had reached the central part of the island and was passing the chapel, it let out a long, muffled whistle blast and set course for Quebec. Then I fell apart and cried my teenaged heart out.

As I was walking by the school after Mass, my aunt stopped me. "Why didn't you come to see Éméril off and wish him a safe trip?" she asked me. I shrugged and said nothing. She let it go at that. She must have understood, just like Johnny — Éméril's father — who, when giving me a loaf of bread that morning, had said to me in a low voice, "A year isn't so long, you know. He'll be back for summer vacation."

Time kept passing. I stayed on the island, and Auntie saw to my education. Always in my mind, Éméril's image was smiling at me. Then, without any warning, Papa, dear Papa, died on July 5, 1916. This was the first cruel hardship of my happy, carefree youth. Sixteen is young to lose one's father. I was old enough, however, to understand that death is final and that Papa was gone forever — he was not coming back for summer vacation. My brothers, bless their little hearts, cried of course, but they did not fully realize what had happened.

We had to leave the island. Mother placed my brothers Gustave and Isidore in the St. Joseph hospice in Lévis. Léon pursued his studies at the Juvenate in Ottawa. Mother found a job with the newspaper *Le Soleil*, where she worked as a proofreader for twenty years. I felt that leaving the island meant dying. Then I had an incredible opportunity; I was offered a job teaching on Ile Sainte-Marguerite.

At the end of the school year, that is to say at the beginning of July, I went from Ile Sainte-Marguerite to Grosse Ile. Mother and my brothers joined me there for a Mass marking the anniversary of Papa's funeral. We stayed with Mr. and Mrs. Masson for a few days. Éméril was already there for his summer vacation. Then we left Grosse Ile for good.

In my book of life, one chapter had come to an end and my thoughts were those of the poet:

The book of life surpasses all others
We cannot close it or open it at will
The endearing passage we cannot read twice
And the fatal page by itself turns
We would like to go back to the page where we love
But the page where we die is already before us.

Lamartine

I was going to live in Quebec with my mother and brothers. You will never know just how lost, disoriented, crushed, wounded, and disillusioned I was when I arrived in the city. Imagine a fish you would try to keep in a bird cage! I wanted air, water, space. I needed the sky, the tides, the sea breezes, the little blue islands, the moonlight.

I missed my little chapel, Johnny Masson's bakery, the birds singing, the bright flowers, the butterflies, the thick white snow, the light that suffused everything. I did not understand that people could be strangers to one another, that we had to lock the doors at night and be wary of one and all. It was no longer the islanders' way of thinking: nice, simple, open, and transparent — it was already no longer as *in my day*.

One thing only gave me comfort and strength — thinking about Éméril. I knew he was lonely too in Ottawa and I prayed for him. When he passed through Quebec on his way to the university in September or to the island in June, he would stop by to say hello, a brief half hour visit.

After Éméril had graduated, he temporarily took charge of a farm Johnny Masson had obtained for Arthur, Éméril's brother. Arthur was studying at the agricultural school in St. Anne de la Pocatière. I found out only in November that Éméril was in St. Clothilde, when he wrote to me for my birthday on November 28, 1920.

On the occasion of a gathering, the Masson families decided to celebrate Mr. and Mrs. Johnny Masson's silver wedding anniversary in July 1922, while the children were out of school. Passing through Quebec one day, Johnny had said to Mother, "Éméril and Jeannette could get married on the day we celebrate our silver wedding on Grosse Ile, if you agree." And thus our wedding date was set for that summer, but Heaven must have decided that the time had not come yet. On March 31, 1922, Johnny Masson had a fatal accident.

After his father's death, Arthur did not want to take over the farm intended for him. As Mrs. Masson and her children had to leave the island, they all moved to the farm. It fell to Éméril to help his mother raise the children.

We did not see much of each other during the following years. Occasionally, Éméril came to Quebec on business and stopped by our place for a little while. And I went to St. Clothilde for a visit during the vacation. Then one day, Éméril wrote to Mother to tell her that things were not too bad on the farm; he would still have to look after his family, of course, but with God's help, he believed he could now start a home and family of his own despite the heavy responsibilities he had taken on. So if she agreed, we could get married.

On November 25, 1925, at the Basilica in Quebec, Father Paré, our former pastor on Grosse Ile who had known us as children, blessed our union. Éméril had his brother Henri as a witness and I had my brother Isidore. Also in attendance at the ceremony were Mother, my young brother Gustave, and Cécile Blais, Henri's wife.

I was wearing a brown velvet dress, which I had made myself, with a white guipure collar. I had also made the hat, of the same material as the dress. A small reception took place at the Vekemans' place, 36 Notre Dame Street in Quebec's Lower-Town (this house is now a museum). Aunt Eugénie, our teacher on Grosse Ile, had set the table. Grandmother Rousseau, ninety-nine years old, seemed happy for me and trilled a little song. On the menu: stuffed roasted goose with vegetables, ham, and tarts, all dishes which I had prepared myself. There were also Grandma Rousseau's own little cakes and a big wedding cake given by Mrs. Caron of *Le Courrier de Montmagny*, the godmother of my brother Gustave and the sister of Mr. Nicole at whose house Grosse Ile's boatmen stopped to warm themselves when they crossed over to Montmagny in winter. She was a friend of the Massons' and the Vekemans'.

For the honeymoon, we simply left for St. Clothilde (Arthabaska County) with Éméril's brother Henri, his wife Cécile, and their two children, Pierre and Kiki. Two days later, Joseph and Alexandre Hamel, our old neighbors on Grosse Ile, came to celebrate the occasion, and everyone up and down the road joined us for a very nice evening. And then followed fifty-five years of everyday living.

And so ended the book entitled "Jeannette Vekeman." Another book, its pages blank, remained to be written...

There you have it, our story. Just as in a fairy tale, the prince married the pretty shepherdess. They had many children and lived happily ever after, reaching a ripe old age.

You wanted me to tell you our love's story. It is not as extraordinary as you expected, but if you find as much happiness as we have, then you will have all you can wish for.

I pay tribute to Éméril for his kindness, his courage, and his understanding.

Pilgrimage to our childhood island. What will we find on Grosse Ile after more than fifty years away?

Nothing has changed. Éméril and I in 1974.

EPILOGUE

Éméril and I went back to Grosse Ile in 1974. Nothing had changed. We then understood that we had lived, not only with our memories, but also with the true meaning of life, which the island had taught us.

I planted a young maple tree there and brought back an oak sapling for my garden. Sitting on the grass on the spot where my childhood house stood long ago, I gathered life by the handfuls in the shape of beautiful wild flowers. The gentle sea breeze, together with the blazing sun, reminded me that man is the heartbeat of the earth — had Éméril and I forgotten that? Whenever I had doubts or felt like giving up during those fifty years of dedication, suppression, trials, and even humiliations — which were also years of happiness with you my children — the island imparted its wisdom to me, a wisdom which could not be false.

That year, during our visit to the island, Éméril and I nodded imperceptibly, laughing at our sorrows. We can honestly say, "We have no regrets."

We are eighty-two years old, or so men say. But we are in fact ageless. Hand in hand, the two of us have only just begun to live out our blue islands surrounded by the clamor of the waves.

An infinity of eternities will not be time enough for us to live out those days of light.

Jeannette Vekeman Masson

WHAT WILL BECOME OF GROSSE ILE?

In my grandmother's heart, it is my wish that the immigrants who lie buried on Grosse Ile not be disturbed. For the most part, they were fleeing from poverty and searching for a promised land. They found it on the Quarantine Island. There they rest in an enchanting, quiet place; we must not disturb their dreams.

I also hope the government will respect Grosse Ile's serenity so there will always be a tranquil place for people to think and find the true meaning of life.

It was this meaning that the Massons of the island had found. They deserve special attention — even if it is only the upkeep of their tombstones. We owe the same consideration to Papa, the employees, and the children forever resting in the lower cemetery.

May the future of my dear Grosse Ile mirror its past as *IN MY DAY.*

I would like to end this story with the moving testimonial of my granddaughter Moïra Dompierre who, at the age of fourteen, had a collection of poems entitled UN SOUFFLE DE TERRE published by Les Éditions Le Livre du Pays.

While reading your manuscript, Grandmother, I have grasped everything that you have harbored in your heart, trying to offer us your thoughts and your island's happiness. With one breath of your past, you make us understand that life does not die but lives on through a breath of earth.

In the name of all your readers and in the name of your children and grandchildren, I give you this poem I wrote in August 1979 while sailing on the river near your islands.

Picturesque
Of Mountains and water
As far
As the eye can see

Picturesque
Of rock
Surrounded
By enchanted water

Picturesque
Of grey
Of blue
Of those hidden
Countries

Picturesque
Of a country
Lonely
But rejoicing

Picturesque
Of a scenery
To be savored
Of a wisdom
To be discovered

Born of those
Mist-colored
Islands
We have discovered
Ourselves to be
People of happiness

Moïra

CALENDAR

1831. Because of the Asiatic cholera epidemic ravaging Europe and of the imminent arrival of thousands of immigrants, Canadian authorities are worried. The facilities of Pointe de Lévis, under the superintendence of Dr. Van Iffland, are deemed insufficient and are too close to populated centers.

Admiral Bayfield designates Grosse Ile as a good site for a quarantine station. Uninhabited and isolated from populated areas, the island offers remarkable mooring possibilities.

1832. The government of Lower Canada requisitions Grosse Ile, the property of Notary Bernier of Château-Richer, to establish a quarantine station.

A garrison made up of two infantry regiments, one Royal Artillery detachment, and several doctors is sent to Grosse Ile under the command of Captain Reid of the 32nd Regiment. The sanitary installations are under the supervision of a superintendent assisted by a surgeon. Each immigrant must undergo a thorough medical examination. Nourishment must also be provided for all the quarantined people who cannot have any outside contacts as long as there is a risk of contagion. The task is not an easy one.

Given the urgency of the situation, tents are set up until rudimentary hospital sheds can be built. Notary Bernier does not allow the government to cut wood on Grosse Ile, so all the necessary lumber has to be shipped in.

While under construction, the Protestant chapel is swept off its foundations by a gust of wind and is raised again on the very spot to which the wind has carried it.

1832. A total of 61,800 immigrants arrive in Canada from England and Ireland. Of these, 51,146 are examined at the Grosse Ile quarantine station.

1833. The Grosse Ile station receives 21,732 immigrants. Of these, 239 are hospitalized and must be quarantined; 159 suffer from fever, thirty-four from smallpox, and forty-six from other diseases. The number of deaths is twenty-seven.

1834. The opening entry of Grosse Ile's first official register is that of a baptism. On May 25, Father J.B. McMahon baptizes William Joice, son of Patrick Joice and Mary Mahoney. Godfather and godmother: John Wallahon and Mary Murry.

The number of immigrants examined is 30,945. Of these, 844 are admitted to the quarantine hospital. Of the 264 deaths, 159 are attributed to cholera, sixty-eight to the fevers, and thirty-seven to smallpox.

1836. Notary Bernier and his tenant, Pierre Duplain, who worked a farm on Grosse Ile, finally receive some compensation from the government.

From the beginning, the Quarantine Island had Catholic and Protestant missions, each with a chapel for worship. The Catholic mission was sponsored by the Society for the Propagation of the Faith, while the Church Society provided funds for the Protestant mission.

The Protestant chapel

1837. Jacque Vézina presents an estimate for the building of an addition to the already existing Catholic chapel. (Archives Diocese of St. Anne de la Pocatière)

1838. The government grants a piece of land for a chapel, a cemetery, and a garden. The above-mentioned Vézina does the work on the chapel before the summer. (Archives Diocese of St. Anne de la Pocatière)

1845. Famine is rampant in Ireland. The British government refuses to help.

1846. The weakened Irish population is penniless. The most fortunate set sail for the United States, avoiding Canada which is a British colony.

The winter in Europe is the worst since the beginning of the century. Doctors warn the authorities that such a state of starvation can result in an epidemic. The British see this as a unique opportunity to people an uninviting colony — Canada. The Irish would rather go to the United States, but the Americans are not very interested in welcoming poor immigrants who carry ship fever.

1847. Anything which can be called a ship is mobilized. The fare from Ireland to Quebec, three pounds sterling, is often paid by the government or landlords eager to get rid of their tenants.

The voyage can last from six weeks to three months. The people are crammed in the ships' holds where there is neither light nor fresh air. Water and food are rationed. Neither age, nor sex, nor decency is respected. Hygiene is nonexistent.

1847. The British do not see fit to warn the Canadians about the extent of the immigration movement. Dr. Douglas, the man in charge of the Grosse Ile quarantine station, warns the authorities that, according to his sources, thousands of Irish are getting ready to leave their country. There are only two hundred available beds at the station.

May 17. Three centimeters of ice still cover the St. Lawrence when the first ship, the *Syria*, drops anchor near Grosse Ile. Of the two hundred and forty-one passengers on board, one hundred must be landed to be put in isolation.

170

May 19. Eight ships arrive with 430 sick passengers on board. The quarantine station is understaffed, the hospital is short of beds, and there are no medicines to treat ship fever patients.

May 20. Thirty ships full of immigrants lie at anchor at Grosse Ile. Of the 12,512 passengers who set sail, 777 are reported to have died during the voyage and been buried at sea, while 459 bodies still remain aboard the ships at anchor.

Food supplies pose a serious problem. Drinking water is in short supply because the river all around the island is contaminated by the refuse of the waiting ships. Boats such as the *Erin's Queen* and the *Triton* are nothing short of foul smelling, floating charnel houses when they arrive.

May 31. A letter from Dr. Douglas is read before the Canadian Parliament by Robert Christie. The quarantine station's superintendent asks that the island be under military watch and that the authorities make certain improvements.

June 15. The authorization to build more sheds is received while about a hundred ships lie at anchor near the island. The Catholic and the Protestant chapels are already being used as hospitals.

A great many doctors, male and female nurses, as well as Catholic and Protestant clergymen come to help the afflicted. They are not spared by contagion. Several die. Those who risk their lives receive only meagre wages of seventeen shillings a day.

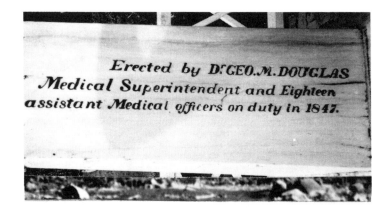

Erected by Dr. GEO. M. DOUGLAS Medical Superintendent and Eighteen assistant Medical officers on duty in 1847.

The pestilence does not spare the ships' crews either. One ship enters the fairway with a white flag raised. Only the captain and his mate are still alive. They die shortly after their arrival.

Contaminated ships must be disinfected. The holds must be whitewashed with quicklime before the ships are allowed to proceed toward Quebec.

July.   The temperature rises to 37° Celsius. Drinking water is in even shorter supply. There are six hundred orphans and two thousand sick on the island. Some doctors and priests die.

In mid-July, the idea of an effective quarantine is given up. It is physically impossible to implement isolation measures. A great many patients must be transported to the Marine Hospital in Quebec where one thousand and forty-one immigrants will eventually die. Some of the city's residents fall sick.

Ship inspections are ineffective. The pestilence spreads to Quebec, then to Montreal. At Pointe St. Charles, where the immigrants bound for Montreal land, six thousand Irish fall prey to the pestilence.

August 28.   Work is completed on huge, hastily built sheds to accommodate three thousand patients. The sick still housed in tents are moved there.

September 12.   The two small chapels become places of worship once more.

October 28. The quarantine station is closed. The navigation season is drawing to an end and no more ships are expected. Father McGauran is the last to leave the island, on board the *Alliance* which carries the last of the immigrants. Six of them die on the way to nearby Quebec. Interestingly, that Irish-born priest had contracted the fever while caring for his brothers. Once cured he had returned to Grosse Ile to pursue his work.

November. Dr. Douglas, the quarantine station superintendent, describes the horrors of this ghastly season. He bears eloquent testimony before a House Committee making inquiries into the matter. He calculates that eight thousand immigrants were buried at sea and that 5,424 Irish died on Grosse Ile.

1847. During the course of the year, 106,000 immigrants arrive in Canada; 68,106 of them passed through Grosse Ile before the station closed for the season. Of the latter group, 8,691 were hospitalized; 8,639 were sick with fever and fifty-two had smallpox. In addition to the quarantine stations, hospitals all the way from Halifax, Quebec, Montreal, up to Toronto and Sarnia have to care for some one thousand nine hundred patients. The death toll is 17,300, representing seventeen percent of the total number of immigrants.

The 1847 Irish immigration will probably go down in human history as one of the most important events of the nineteenth century. During that one year, two hundred and twenty-one ships sail from Ireland, one hundred and forty from England, forty-two from Scotland, and thirty-six from Germany.

1847. Dr. Douglas and his staff of eighteen doctors erect a marble monument whose inscription reads: "**In this secluded spot lie the mortal remains of 5,424 persons who flying from Pestilence and Famine in Ireland in the year 1847 found in America but a Grave.**"

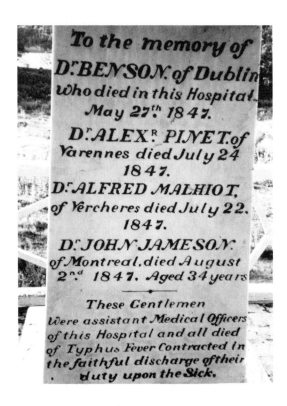

This monument also honors the memory of Dr. Benson of Dublin who died on May 27, 1847; Dr. Alex Pinet of Varennes who died on July 24; Dr. Alfred Malhiot of Verchères who died on July 22, and Dr. Jameson of Montreal who died on August 2 at the age of thirty-four. Members of the hospital staff, they all died of typhus fever contracted while ministering to the sick.

The same monument honors the memory of Dr. Alfred Panet, also a medical officer of the quarantine hospital, who died of cholera in July 1834, and Dr. Robert Christie, assistant medical officer, who died of typhus fever on July 2, 1847. (Archives St. Luke's parish)

The upper wharf

1847.   Mr. W. Patton of St. Thomas builds a wharf at the upper end of Grosse Ile.

1847.   A road is laid to link the various groups of buildings.

1849.   Three cannons are set up on the island to ensure that all ships obey the injunction to stop for inspection.

1849 or 1850.   A school is fitted out and a teacher comes to the island to teach the employees' children.

1857. The Imperial government transfers all its rights over the quarantine station to the Canadian government. From then on, the island falls under the jurisdiction of the Department of Agriculture. The military garrison, under the command of Lieutenant Noble, leaves the island.

1857. A Chief Medical Officer is now in charge of the quarantine station. His title is that of superintendent and he is the sole master on the island.

1863. Édouard Masson arrives on Grosse Ile. He is seasonally employed by the government as a baker and a carter. He earns fifty dollars a month. Mr. Masson will continue working for the government on the island for forty-two years. (Jeannette Vekeman)

1866. A wharf is built in the lower section of the island by Laberge and Co. of Quebec.

1869. On October 25, the quarters of the Medical Superintendent and all his papers are destroyed by fire. In a report, Dr. Montizambert says that a faulty chimney is to blame for the fire.

1870. The archdiocese of Quebec receives a letter from Grosse Ile's missionary stating that the buildings are run-down and that a bilingual teacher is urgently needed. (Archives Diocese of St. Anne de la Pocatière)

1874. A letter from the archdiocese, dated July 1, mentions the need to build a new chapel. (Archives Diocese of St. Anne de la Pocatière)

1874. A letter from Father Laliberté attests that another Catholic chapel will be built, but on a new site more readily accessible to all. (Archives Diocese of St. Anne de la Pocatière)

1874. Édouard Masson now resides on Grosse Ile year-round.

1875. In a letter, the archdiocese gives authorization to build the new chapel. (Archives Diocese of St. Anne de la Pocatière)

1875. Mr. Richard of Quebec makes repairs on the upper wharf.

1877. The Society for the Propagation of the Faith donates some accessories for the new presbytery and chapel. (These two buildings are still standing today). An inscription on the chapel bell states that it was made in Vimy in 1809. (Archives Diocese of St. Anne de la Pocatière)

1877. Pierre (Pit) Masson, Édouard's son, is born on the island. (Jeannette Vekeman)

1878. A fire destroys three buildings and part of the quarantine station's records. This fire is all the more deplorable because there is reason to believe that it was deliberately set.

1889. The island is provided with a new ambulance. [It is still preserved in the old hospital laundry.] (Public Archives)

1889. A total of 50,879 people are checked for yellow fever.

September 6. Members of the Provincial Board of Health come to the station on an official visit. They are Dr. Lachapelle, President, Dr. Lemieux, Dr. Garneau, Dr. Paquet, Dr. Craik, and Dr. Pelletier, Secretary. (Public Archives)

September 16. The SS. *Alberta*, arriving at Grosse Ile from the Philippines, reports Asiatic cholera aboard. (Public Archives)

1894. On March 5, a case of leprosy is reported on board the *Balwinson*, coming from Iceland.

1896. Pierre (Pit) Masson replaces his father Édouard as ambulance driver, carter, and boatman for the quarantine station. (Lucienne Masson of Montmagny, Pierre Masson's daughter)

1897. Johnny Masson, Édouard's son, marries Éléonore Delorme on the island. (Registers of St. Luke's parish)

1897. The Ancient Order of Hibernians organizes a pilgrimage to commemorate the fiftieth anniversary of the 1847 epidemic.

1898. On April 19, the island employees receive a pay raise. Édouard Masson earns twenty dollars more a month.

1899. Sir Wilfrid Laurier appoints Dr. Martineau superintendent of Grosse Ile. (Jeanne Martineau-Boulet's book on her family)

1905. Johnny Masson replaces his father as baker. (Éméril Masson)

1906. April 1. Gustave Vekeman arrives on Grosse Ile to work as an interpreter. (Jeannette Vekeman)

1906. On September 6, the teacher, Miss Pelletier, disappears, never to be found again. (letter from G. Vekeman, dated September 14, in *Le Courrier de Montmagny*, vol. 23, no. 36, p. 4)

1907. Gustave Vekeman's family arrives on the island at the end of April.[1]

May. On the way back from Montmagny, three men die when the yacht provided for the islanders' use is shipwrecked.

June. The steamer *Contest* is replaced by the *Alice*.

1909. On August 15, consecration of the Irish monument. Surmounted by a Celtic cross, the monument is forty-eight feet high. On its base, three inscriptions, in English, French, and Gaelic, explain why the monument was erected. A fourth inscription lists the names of the forty-four Catholic priests who came to Grosse Ile in 1847 and 1848.

1911. The *Polana* replaces the *Challenger* as the steamer at the immigrants' disposal.

1913. A two hundred by fifty foot extension is added to the upper wharf.

1913. In August, lights are installed along the island's road.

1915. Grosse Ile is connected by telephone to the mainland.

1915. Birth of Freddy Masson, Pierre (Pit) Masson's son.

1916. Death of Gustave Vekeman on the island at the age of seventy-five.

1922. Johnny Masson dies in an accident on the island at the age of fifty-four.

1925. The Medical Superintendent's house is destroyed by fire.

---

[1] Information about the period from 1907 to 1925 was provided by Jeannette Vekeman.

1926. The lower wharf is destroyed during a heavy storm. It will not be rebuilt.

1928. Brother Marie-Victorin spends the summer on Grosse Ile to collect plants for botanical study. (Lucienne Masson)

1929. Pierre (Pit) Masson's salary is reduced from eighty to sixty dollars a month. (Lucienne Masson)

1929. Death of the quarantine station's superintendent, Dr. Martineau. Activity on the island slows down considerably. (Lucienne Masson)

1935. From February 3 to April 13, an ice-bridge links Grosse Ile to Ile Sainte-Marguerite. (Lucienne Masson)

1935. On May 6, Captain Ludger Fournier pins a silver medal on Pierre (Pit) Masson's chest on the occasion of King George V's silver jubilee. Pierre Masson will eventually spend forty-five years working for the quarantine service. (Lucienne Masson)

Pit Masson and his wife and other employees after the award ceremony

1936. The station is run by Dr. C.H. Laurin and Dr. Chrétien. A qualified staff remains on hand, prepared for all contingencies, in case contagion were to be found amongst passengers bound for Quebec.

1937.   After 105 years in operation, the quarantine station is closed. The various immigration, hygiene, inspection, and quarantine services are now centralized in the Quebec harbor. Two caretakers, Mr. Pierre Masson and Mr. N. Lachance, remain on the island. (Jeannette Vekeman and Lucienne Masson)

The island still boasts several clinic hotels capable of accommodating 1,080 people, a 130–bed hospital, a well-equipped laboratory, a generator, a disinfection shed, a presbytery and a Catholic chapel, a Protestant chapel and a rectory, as well as various accommodations for the remaining thirteen families.

In October, much of the furniture is moved from the buildings to Quebec, Halifax, and St. Anne de Bellevue. Only the disinfection shed is left untouched.

1938.   On July 10, the steamer *Druid* brings some thirty people to Grosse Ile for a pilgrimage. Picnics on the island are in fashion during the summer.

August 31.   At the request of the Department of National Defence, an order in council transfers jurisdiction over Grosse Ile to the Department of Public Works. (P.C. 2119)

1943.   On March 2, the Department of National Defence regains control of Grosse Ile and from then on pays for its upkeep. The Department and the United States jointly set up an animal disease research center on the island. This project is named Project "R." (File 1681)

1946.   On January 28, as a result of Project "R," the development of a rinderpest vaccine is announced after a series of successful laboratory and field tests. The Department of National Defence maintains the laboratory and its research program for an extended period of time, paying expenses of sixteen thousand dollars a month. A sum of ninety-six thousand dollars is granted for the production of the vaccine. (R.P.T. 297757B National Defence and Agriculture)

1947.   On Wednesday, November 19, His Excellency the Governor General in Council, on recommendation of the Minister of National Defence, and in accordance with the provisions of the Official Secrets Act (chapter 49 of the Statutes of Canada, 1939), orders that Grosse Ile, County of Montmagny, Province of Quebec, be declared a prohibited place within the meaning of the said Act.

This order is given because of the highly secret nature of the bacteriological research conducted on the island and on the recommendation of the Dominion Animal Pathologist who considers the actual soil of the island to be toxic in certain areas.

This prohibition also aims at maintaining and protecting the island's valuable installations which, it is felt, should be kept in good repair for possible future use. Because there is a fire hazard on the heavily wooded island, this measure is also meant to ward off trespassers who might damage or jeopardize the installations of the Department of National Defence. The staff of three caretakers is felt to be inadequate to protect them. (P.C. 4728)

1947. Pierre (Pit) Masson leaves Grosse Ile at the age of seventy. (Lucienne Masson)

1952. In April, a Canadian Press release originating from Ottawa mentions that the Canadian government is having bacteriological and biological warfare experiments conducted on Grosse Ile.

1952. In the spring, the Ottawa newspaper *Le Droit* refers to "*the most secret research projects of the defence program, which pertain to biological or bacteriological warfare.*"

According to the same newspaper, Dr. Solandt, chairman of the Defence Research Board, has revealed that "*these research projects are part of a program whose aim is to give Canada the means to defend itself or strike back in the event of a chemical or bacteriological war. Scientists are conducting, on Grosse Ile, experiments which they would be reluctant to undertake on the mainland.*"

In another article, *Le Droit* comments on the University of Wisconsin's offering China a great many doses of a secret vaccine developed to protect American cattle against viruses of Japanese origin. It seems that the vaccine is one which immunizes against cattle plague, the worst of all cattle diseases. The same article states that this vaccine has been developed by scientists in a secret laboratory on Grosse Ile. (*Le Droit*)

1957. The federal Department of Agriculture is granted the use of Grosse Ile by the Defence Research Board to establish a laboratory for animal virus disease research.

1961. On February 23, the order in council (P.C. 4728) of November 19, 1947, which declared Grosse Ile to be a prohibited place, is amended. The amendment reads as follows: "*This Order does not apply to over-flying aircraft.*"

1965. On February 25, in Ottawa, Mr. Harry Hays, Minister of Agriculture, announces the establishment on Grosse Ile of a maximum security quarantine station for livestock imported from Europe or elsewhere and eventually destined for the American market.

1967. In March, a herd of Charolais cattle is released from Grosse Ile after a period of quarantine. The animals, in excellent health, are shipped to seven Canadian provinces. The two hundred and fifteen head are worth $1,550,000. It is the second shipment of French Charolais since 1900.
Animal virus disease research is still under way on the island.

1968. A fire destroys the hospital and the rear section of the facilities where sick animals were kept. (Freddy Masson, then the island superintendent)

What remains of the hospital.

1968. Grosse Ile becomes a world-famous center for research on animal diseases, especially of viral or exotic origin. Every year, veterinarians from around the world come there to study. The courses are under the supervision of Dr. Julius Frank. The research work done in collaboration with the United States is unique in the world. Some courses offered exclusively to the American military are given there periodically.

Grosse Ile remains off limits to laymen. No one is allowed on the island without a written authorization from Ottawa, and such authorizations are very seldom given.

1978. In the fall, Parks Canada unveils a commemorative plaque commissioned by the Historic Sites and Monuments Board.

1980. In May, Mr. Freddy Masson, the island superintendent, retires thus ending the 117–year presence of the Massons on Grosse Ile.

Freddy Masson

1982. One hundred and fiftieth anniversary of the opening of the quarantine station on Grosse Ile.

1988. August. An agreement is signed by Agriculture Canada and Environment Canada turning over most of the island to Parks Canada.

BIBLIOGRAPHY

Histoire de l'Irlande — Pierre Joannon — Paris.

Le drame de la Grosse-Isle — abbé Adélard Derosiers — 1934 — Soc. Hist. de Montréal.

L'Immigration Irlandaise (1847) — Paul Émile Vaillancourt.

Mémoire sur le Choléra — Ministère de l'agriculture et statistiques (1866).

The Irish Emigration of 1847 and its consequence — Rev. John A. Gallagher C.SS.R., C.C.H.A Annual Report 1935-36

The Grosse-Ile Tragedy — Quebec 1909 — J.A. Jordan.

Four Centuries of Medical History in Canada — Toronto 1928 — Vol. 1 — J.J. Heagerty.

"Grosse-Ile" — Four articles in the *Catholic Record* of London Ont. — April 9 ff. 1892 — by M.J. O'Leary.

La Grosse Île — Montréal — Flaherty.

The Irish in America — N.Y. 1868 — J.F. Maguire.

"L'Île Cimetière" — *Perspective*, 2 mai 1964 — J.J. LeFrançois.

"L'Île de la Quarantaine" — *Le Saint-Laurent et ses Îles* — 1945 — Damase Potvin.

Le Courrier de Montmagny — octobre 1957 — Charles M. LeTarte.

Le Droit — Ottawa — mars-avril 1957.

Québec-Science — 1976.

Archives Archdiocese of Quebec.

Archives Diocese of Ste. Anne de la Pocatière.

National Archives — Quebec — Montreal.

Public Archives — Ottawa.

Parks Canada — Ste. Foy office.

Printed by Éditions Marquis
Montmagny, P.Q.
1989